LAZY INVESTOR SMART INVESTOR

The Secrets to Turning Laziness into Wealth Through the Stock Market, Portfolio Management, and Day Trading

John Bax

Table of Contents

3

Disclaimer

The information provided in this book is for educational purposes only and does not constitute financial advice or a solicitation to invest or engage in speculative activities. The author is not responsible for any financial losses resulting from investments, day trading, or any other speculative activities involving stocks, ETFs, forex, cryptocurrencies, or any other assets discussed in this book. Participating in financial markets, whether through long-term investments or short-term speculation, carries significant risks, and your capital is always at risk.

Always conduct your own research. Don't base your investment or speculative decisions solely on the content of this book. Evaluate your own financial situation, objectives, and risk tolerance before engaging in any financial activity. Take responsibility for your financial decisions and seek professional advice if needed.

About the Author

John Bax is one of our talented authors here at Books Go Publications, where we are dedicated to empowering readers with practical and impactful knowledge. We pride ourselves on a strong reputation for excellence, with numerous bestsellers across a variety of topics. While all our books are available on Amazon, more information about our catalog and authors can be found on our website: www.booksgopublications.com.

John Bax is a seasoned investor and trader with extensive experience in both traditional and emerging financial markets. In 2019, he founded "Crypto Go", a vibrant community dedicated to providing individuals with the knowledge and tools to navigate the crypto world. John views crypto as a revolutionary asset class that combines innovation with unique investment opportunities. He is also the author of the bestselling book *"Cryptocurrency Investing: Step-By-Step Guide to Benefit from Crypto by Investing Long Term and Trading Short Term Following the Smart Money Strategies on DeFi Blockchains"*. Translated into four languages, this book has helped thousands of readers confidently navigate the complexities of the crypto world. It is available on Amazon. To learn more about Crypto Go, visit www.thecryptogo.com.

Crypto Go is well-known for its highly successful service for "lazy" investors and traders: *"Crypto Go Wealth Accelerator."* Trusted by thousands of investors and traders worldwide, this exclusive program offers an innovative approach to maximizing returns in two key areas: profiting from short-term crypto speculation and building long-term wealth through strategic ETF portfolio investments.

Designed for those who want results instantly and effortlessly, *Crypto Go Wealth Accelerator* provides optimized strategies and a lazy model that minimizes effort while maximizing efficiency.

Crypto Go Wealth Accelerator **is available only a few times a year for new members, and it comes with an unbeatable guarantee—if you don't see results within 15 days, you can request a full refund, no questions asked. Discover more by scanning this QR code:**

You can also find additional details about the program at the end of the book in the chapter titled "Extra: Crypto Go Wealth Accelerator".

3 Free Bonuses for You

Welcome, dear reader, and thank you for placing your trust in this book. I hope it exceeds your expectations and offers valuable insights into building and managing a long-term investment portfolio, as well as navigating the fast-paced world of short-term speculation. Above all, my aim is to equip you with the knowledge and confidence to approach both investing and trading with clarity and independence.

To show my gratitude, I am excited to offer you three exclusive bonuses to complement what you'll learn in this book.

Bonus 1: Free eBook "10 Mistakes to Avoid in Your Investment Portfolio"

Building and managing a successful investment portfolio is no easy task. Even experienced investors can fall into common traps that harm their long-term returns. This bonus eBook highlights the 10 most frequent mistakes people make when constructing and managing their portfolios. More importantly, it offers practical advice to help you avoid these pitfalls. Consider it a valuable companion to the chapters in this book dedicated to portfolio building and management.

Bonus 2: Free eBook "10 Mistakes to Avoid in Day Trading"

Day trading can be exciting, but it's also one of the most demanding ways to make money in the markets. Without proper preparation and discipline, traders often fall into critical mistakes that can quickly deplete their accounts. This bonus eBook explores the 10 most common pitfalls in day trading. Whether you're just starting out or have some experience, this guide will help you trade more effectively and avoid the traps that hinder so many traders.

Bonus 3: This Week's Hottest Crypto Pick From Our Expert Analysts

As part of the exclusive services offered to *Crypto Go Wealth Accelerator* members, we provide weekly in-depth analysis of high-potential crypto assets with strong short-term growth prospects. These insights are delivered through our premium Telegram channel, "Crypto Go Analysis." Our expert analysts conduct weekly on-chain and fundamental analyses to provide our members with the highest potential tokens in the crypto market. If any of these terms are unfamiliar, you can deepen your understanding of the crypto world by reading our bestselling book, *"Cryptocurrency Investing"*. Access to this weekly analysis Telegram channel of ours comes at a cost, of course. You will find more details at the end of this book. However, by purchasing this book, you are entitled to receive the analysis of the latest asset selected by our experts; a unique opportunity to discover the latest cryptocurrency that our analysts have identified for its short-term growth potential.

I would like to emphasize that although we are committed to providing you with a very accurate analysis, this is not a financial advice. It is an opportunity for you to get an inside view of the latest "hot pick" from our team of experts. Don't miss the chance to get a free preview of what *Crypto Go Wealth Accelerator* has to offer.

Download Your Three Free Bonuses Here!

You can download these three free bonuses by scanning the following QR code from your smartphone:

Introduction

For decades, we've been conditioned to believe a simple narrative: the harder you work, the more success you'll achieve. This mindset is particularly ingrained in the financial world, where many assume that success hinges on relentless market monitoring, analyzing endless streams of data, and mastering intricate strategies. But the truth is, when it comes to investing and trading, working harder doesn't always mean working smarter. In fact, excessive effort often leads to wasted time, heightened stress, and results that fall short of expectations. Consider the realms of stock market investing and day trading. Many people assume that making countless trades or employing intricate strategies will automatically yield better returns. However, studies show the opposite: simplicity often triumphs over complexity. Strategies that require less effort frequently deliver superior results, especially over the long term[1].

This is where the concept of "lazy" investing and trading comes in. Being lazy doesn't mean being ignorant or careless; it means adopting strategies that optimize your time, energy, and resources to achieve exceptional outcomes. Often, these approaches outperform the exhausting, overly complicated methods many investors and traders adopt. Whether you're completely new to investing and trading or have some experience, this guide is designed to provide you with not just the basics, but a clear roadmap to success tailored to a "lazy yet effective" mindset.

---

[1] **Malkiel, B. G. (2020).** *A Random Walk Down Wall Street: The Time-Tested Strategy for Successful Investing.* W.W. Norton & Company.

This book is divided into four main parts, plus an extra:

Part I: The Investment & Trading Essentials the Lazy Investor Must Know

Part I introduces the core principles of investing and trading. It begins by addressing the importance of overcoming the fear of losing money, understanding the impact of inflation, and planning for long-term goals like retirement. It then explores essential financial concepts, including the difference between investing and speculating, assessing risk tolerance, and harnessing the power of compound interest. Finally, it provides a preliminary introduction to the stock market, value investing, portfolio management, and day trading, all concepts that will be explored in greater depth throughout the book.

Part II: Value Investing and ETFs

Part II explores two key components of the investment landscape: value investing and Exchange-Traded Funds (ETFs). It begins with an in-depth look at value investing. You'll uncover the ten core principles of value investing, learn how to use key metrics to identify undervalued assets, and discover a step-by-step process for building a complete value investing strategy. This section also addresses the challenges of value investing. The latter half focuses on ETFs, explaining what they are, their essential features, and the various types available. It emphasizes how ETFs can streamline portfolio diversification, offering a straightforward and efficient way to achieve steady returns without the complexities of individual stock selection.

Part III: The Lazy Investor's Portfolio

Part III provides a practical framework for constructing and managing an investment portfolio tailored to the needs of a lazy investor. This part begins by explaining the principles of building a balanced portfolio, focusing on the risk-reward ratio, asset correlation, and diversification. The second part introduces Dollar-Cost Averaging (DCA) as a powerful and stress-free approach to steadily grow your savings over time. It also covers essential topics like portfolio rebalancing to maintain alignment with investment goals and strategies for achieving tax efficiency.

Part IV: The Lazy Trader's Strategies

Part IV delves into the world of day trading, providing a thorough exploration of its mechanics, strategies, and inherent challenges. It begins by introducing the fundamentals of day trading, including the most suitable assets and an overview of technical analysis. You will then discover five popular day trading strategies and learn how to execute trades effectively. The second section offers a critical perspective on day trading, highlighting why it often fails to meet the expectations of most traders. Finally, this part presents smarter and more sustainable alternatives for short-term speculation. These solutions allow you to engage with the market in a way that minimizes the intense effort and risks typically associated with traditional day trading.

Extra: Crypto Go Wealth Accelerator

At the end of this book, you'll discover something special—our exclusive *Crypto Go Wealth Accelerator* program, designed to make both short-term speculation and long-term investing more accessible and, most importantly, more profitable for you. This service is tailored for those who want effective, stress-free tools without sacrificing time or energy.

I encourage you to read this book sequentially rather than skipping around. Whether your aim is to build long-term wealth or explore short-term speculative strategies, this guide is designed to equip you with the knowledge and confidence to succeed without unnecessary effort or overcomplication. Before we begin, I'd like to express my heartfelt thanks to my incredible team of financial analysts, traders, consultants, and investment specialists who contributed to this book. Their insights and support were invaluable in helping me convey these concepts as effectively as possible. Happy reading!

PART I: The Investment & Trading Essentials the Lazy Investor Must Know

Chapter 1: Breaking Down the Barriers to Investing

Why Most People Never Start Investing

Investing is one of the most effective ways to build wealth, yet so many people hesitate to take the first step. This hesitation stems from more than just procrastination or lack of ambition; it's often a combination of fear, misconceptions, and the overwhelming complexity of the financial world that holds people back before they even begin. For many, the idea of investing feels like stepping into an alien world. Terms like stocks, bonds, ETFs, DCA, and investment portfolio are thrown around, creating a sense of intimidation. If you've never been exposed to these concepts, they can seem complex and confusing. Financial news and charts only add to the anxiety, making it easy to believe that investing is something only experts can do. This fear of the unknown creates a mental block that prevents people from even exploring their investment options.

Another major obstacle is the fear of losing money. This concern is not unfounded. Markets can be volatile, and stories of stock crashes or financial catastrophes are all too common. It's easy to focus on the risks rather than the potential rewards. People often imagine the worst-case scenario: their savings wiped out, their hard-earned money disappearing overnight. The truth is that while market fluctuations are a reality, investing wisely and with a long-term perspective can significantly reduce these risks[2]. Still, the fear of failure looms large and stops many before they've even begun. Misconceptions about the amount of money needed to start investing also play a big role. Many people believe that investing is only for the wealthy or those with many thousands or millions of dollars to spare. This simply isn't true. But this misconception creates a psychological barrier: why bother learning about investing if you feel like you can't afford to participate? Ironically, the digital age has made the problem even worse. While we now have unprecedented access to information, the sheer abundance of resources on investing often leads to analysis paralysis. The overwhelming number of learning options can leave people feeling stuck and unsure of where to begin. Should you invest in individual stocks, mutual funds, or ETFs? What about crypto and forex? The overload of choices often leads people to put off decisions indefinitely.

Perfectionism is another hidden obstacle. Many people wait for the perfect time to start investing - when they've saved a little more, when they've learned more, or when they feel more confident. The reality is that there's never a perfect time to start. Markets are unpredictable, and life is full of financial uncertainties. Waiting for the ideal time often means missing out on the compounding benefits of starting early (we will discuss compound interest later). The sooner you start, the more time your investments have to grow. It's better to take small, imperfect steps than to stand still. Finally, many people feel they simply don't have the time to invest. Life is busy, and the thought of spending hours researching stocks, analyzing trends, and monitoring markets is daunting. This is where the lazy investor philosophy comes into play. Investing and trading don't have to consume all your free time, as you'll discover in this book. All of these obstacles are real, but they are not insurmountable. The fact that you're reading this book shows that you're already taking steps to overcome them.

---

[2] **Bogle, J.C. (2017).** *The Little Book of Common Sense Investing: The Only Way to Guarantee Your Fair Share of Stock Market Returns.* Wiley.

Dealing with the Fear of Losing Money

The fear of losing money is one of the most common barriers to investing or trading. It's a natural reaction, hardwired into us as human beings. After all, money represents security, effort, and freedom. The thought of risking it can feel reckless, even terrifying. But understanding where this fear comes from and how to manage it is key to becoming a successful, confident investor. At its core, the fear of losing money is deeply emotional. For many, this fear is compounded by a lack of control. When you invest or trade, you're putting your money in the hands of the market—a vast, unpredictable ecosystem influenced by countless factors, from politics to the global economy. This uncertainty can make even the most rational person hesitate. But here's the reality: life is full of uncertainty. Even keeping your money in cash or a savings account isn't without risk. Inflation gradually erodes your purchasing power, meaning that the money you save today will buy less tomorrow, as we will discuss in the next sub-chapter. Doing nothing is a risk in itself.

A major driver of fear of loss is our brain's natural tendency to avoid pain. Behavioral economists call this "loss aversion," the idea that losses feel more impactful than equivalent gains[3]. For example, losing $100 feels much worse than the joy of gaining $100. This bias makes it harder to take even calculated risks, even when the potential rewards outweigh the losses. It's not just about money. It's about protecting ourselves from emotional pain and regret. Consequently, it's essential to reframe your perspective on loss. The first step toward achieving this is through education, as fear of loss often stems from the unknown. When you don't understand how the markets work, every fluctuation feels like a personal attack on your finances. But with knowledge, you can begin to see the bigger picture. I hope this book will help do just that. Instead of seeing losses as failures, see them as part of the process. Even the best investors and traders in the world experience losses. It's

---

[3] **Kahneman, D. & Tversky, A. (1979).** *Prospect Theory: An Analysis of Decision under Risk.* Econometrica, 47(2), 263–291.

an inevitable part of the journey. What distinguishes successful investors is their ability to stay calm, learn from their mistakes, and stick to their long-term plan. The fear of losing money is natural, but it doesn't have to control you. By educating yourself and keeping the big picture in mind, you can turn this fear into a manageable part of your investing journey.

Inflation: The Silent Wealth Destroyer

When people think about losing money, they often imagine dramatic scenarios: stock market crashes, failed business ventures, or poorly timed investments. But there's a much quieter, more insidious force eroding wealth every day; one that affects everyone, no matter how safe they think their money is. That force is inflation. Inflation is the gradual increase in prices over time that erodes the purchasing power of your money. Simply put, inflation means that the money you have today will buy less in the future. For example, if inflation is 3% per year, something that costs $100 today will cost $103 next year. Over time, this seemingly small change can have a massive impact. At an annual inflation rate of 3%, the value of your money will be cut in half in about 24 years. That's the silent wealth destroyer at work. For many people, inflation is invisible. You don't notice it from day to day, but over months and years it adds up. The price of groceries creeps up, rent goes up, and your favorite coffee costs more than it did last year. These changes are so gradual that they're easy to ignore—until you realize that maybe your salary or savings aren't keeping up. If the money you're earning or saving isn't growing faster than inflation, you're effectively losing purchasing power.

One of the biggest myths about money is that it is "safe" to keep it in a savings account. While savings accounts protect your money from market fluctuations, they do very little to protect it from inflation. Most savings accounts today offer interest rates well below the current rate of inflation, which means your money will lose value even if it sits untouched. A "safe" strategy that involves hoarding cash can, ironically, be one of the riskiest moves you can make. Governments and central banks aim to maintain moderate levels of inflation (typically, close but below 3% annually) in order to keep the economy growing[4]. While controlled inflation is a sign of a healthy economy, it's a double-edged sword for those who aren't prepared. Without a strategy to combat inflation, even the most disciplined savers will find their financial goals slipping further out of reach. One of the most dangerous aspects of inflation is how it undermines long-term financial planning. Imagine you're saving for retirement, and you calculate that you'll need $1 million to live comfortably. If you base that number on today's prices, you're underestimating your future needs. In 20 or 30 years, due to inflation, that same $1 million may have the purchasing power of $500,000 or less. Planning without inflation is like trying to navigate without a map: you're likely to end up far from where you want to be.

So how do you fight back against this silent wealth destroyer? The answer is to make your money work for you. Unlike cash, investments have the potential to grow faster than inflation. Whether you're just starting to invest or looking to refine your strategy, I am sure this book will help you very much. By investing wisely, diversifying your portfolio, and staying disciplined, you can not only protect your money from inflation, but actually grow it over time.

Planning for the Future: Why Retirement Starts Today

Retirement may feel like a distant concern, something to think about "later" when you're older, more established, and closer to the finish line of your career. But here's the uncomfortable truth: the earlier you start planning for retirement, the easier and less stressful the journey will be. Waiting too long to take action is one of the biggest mistakes people make, and it's a costly one. Time is your most powerful ally when it comes to building wealth for the future. It's not just how much money you save; it's how long that money can grow. The longer your investments are allowed to compound, the greater their potential to multiply. Compound interest, often called the "eighth wonder of the

---

[4] **Mishkin, F. S. (2007).** *The Economics of Money, Banking, and Financial Markets.* Pearson Education.

world," works its magic over time. It's the process by which your money earns returns, and those returns then earn returns of their own. The earlier you start, the more opportunities you have for this snowball effect to occur. Delaying even a few years can dramatically reduce the size of your retirement nest egg. We will discuss compound interest in greater details later.

Yet despite the clear benefits of starting early, many people procrastinate. Retirement feels too far away, and there are always more immediate financial priorities like buying a car or saving for a vacation. It's easy to fall into the trap of thinking, "I'll start saving next year," but this mindset can quickly snowball into years of lost opportunity. The reality is that the longer you wait, the harder it is to catch up. Another common barrier is the misconception that you need to be wealthy to start saving for retirement. Many people believe they need to set aside large sums of money to make an impact, but this couldn't be further from the truth. Even small, consistent monthly contributions can grow significantly over time. Thanks to the power of compounding, starting with a modest amount today is far more effective than waiting until you can save a larger sum in the future. Personal investments play a critical role in retirement planning. Stocks, bonds, ETFs and other financial instruments can help grow your wealth over time. The good news is that building and managing an investment portfolio to secure a great retirement doesn't have to be complicated. As you'll discover in this book, with the right strategies and tools, the process can be both simple and effective.

Chapter 2: Financial Basics for Lazy Investors & Traders

Can you help us? If you like the book, please leave a review on Amazon by scanning the following QR code with your smartphone. For you it is a matter of seconds, but for us it is invaluable. Thank you in advance!

If something is not to your liking, please let us know by email at info@thecryptogo.com. We will use your feedback to improve the book.

Also, if you're interested in taking your wealth to the next level, check out *Crypto Go Wealth Accelerator.* It's available only a few times a year. Scan the QR code below to learn more:

Investing vs. Speculating

One of the first concepts a lazy investor or trader needs to grasp is the fundamental difference between investing and speculating. While both involve putting money into financial assets, their goals, approaches, and risks couldn't be more different. Understanding these differences will help you navigate your financial decisions with clarity and purpose. Here are six key differences between investing and speculating that every aspiring investor or trader should know:

1. **Time Horizon.** Investing is an inherently long-term activity. When you invest, you commit to holding an asset for many years, with the expectation that its intrinsic value will increase over time. This patient approach allows your investment to ride out market volatility and benefit from compounding growth. Speculation, on the other hand, operates on a much shorter time horizon. Speculators aim to profit from price movements over varying timeframes, such as months, weeks, or days, with the shortest horizon being day trading, where positions are opened and closed within the same trading day.

2. **Timing and Entry Price.** For investors, the precise timing of the purchase of an asset is less critical. Long-term investors look at the bigger picture, focusing on the asset's potential to grow over the years rather than worrying about short-term price fluctuations. Indeed, investing strategies like dollar-cost averaging (DCA), which we will discuss later, involve investing a fixed amount at regular intervals and help smooth out the effects of market volatility. Speculation, on the other hand, is all about timing. Speculators obsess over entry and exit points because their profits depend on accurately predicting short-term price movements.

3. **Market Direction.** Investing generally depends on a bullish outlook: investors buy assets with the expectation that their value will increase over time. Speculation, on the other hand, offers the opportunity to profit from both rising and falling mar-

kets. By utilizing strategies like short selling or trading derivatives, speculators can capitalize on downward price movements as well as upward trends.

4. **Risk-Return Ratio.** The risk-return (or risk-reward) ratio is a fundamental concept in finance. It reflects the relationship between the potential risk and reward of any investment, trade, or strategy. Typically, the greater the risk associated with an asset, investment, or trade, the higher the potential reward, and vice versa. The overall risk-return ratio of a portfolio depends on the risk-return profiles of the assets it comprises. We will delve deeper into this concept when discussing portfolio creation later in the book. For now, it's important to understand that, in general, investing typically offers a more moderate risk-return ratio compared to short-term speculation. By diversifying a portfolio and holding assets for the long term, investors aim for steady, compounding growth with lower overall risk. Speculation, on the other hand, involves much higher risks in exchange for the possibility of substantial short-term gains. While speculative trades can yield impressive returns in a short time, they also carry the significant possibility of equally substantial losses.

5. **Reasons for Buying and Selling.** The motivation for buying an asset is very different between the two approaches. Investors buy assets because they believe in the intrinsic value or long-term potential of the underlying project, company, or idea. For example, you might invest in a company's stock because you believe it has innovative products that will dominate the market for years to come. Speculators, on the other hand, don't care about the underlying value of an asset; their focus is solely on price movements. They buy or sell based on what market sentiment and/or technical analysis suggest will happen next, often ignoring the fundamental aspects of the asset.

6. **Fundamental vs. Technical Analysis.** Investment decisions are usually based on fundamental analysis, which assesses the intrinsic value of an asset by evaluating its financial health, market potential, and other factors. This type of analysis is particularly relevant for assessing the stocks of specific companies, a

methodology known as value investing. Later in this book, we will explore value investing in detail and how it helps to identify potentially undervalued opportunities in the stock market. Speculation, on the other hand, relies heavily on technical analysis, which studies historical price patterns, trends, and statistical indicators to predict future movements. Fundamental analysis focuses on the "why" behind an asset's value, while technical analysis is more concerned with the "when" of price movements.

This book is designed to guide you in both worlds: long-term investing and short-term speculation, while minimizing effort and maximizing returns. On the investing side, you'll learn how to build a portfolio tailored to your goals and risk tolerance, and how to manage it effectively over time with minimal maintenance. On the speculative side, this book will introduce you to innovative, simplified, and profitable ways to engage in short-term trading.

Risk Tolerance

Understanding your personal risk tolerance is a cornerstone of successful investing. Risk tolerance refers to the amount of uncertainty or potential financial loss you're willing to accept in exchange for the possibility of achieving higher returns. Assessing this tolerance is crucial because it determines not only the types of assets you should include in your portfolio, but also the proportions of each. But how do you assess your risk tolerance? It's not a single number or a rigid formula. It's a nuanced assessment based on multiple factors that vary from person to person. Below, we'll explore the key parameters that can help you determine what level of risk you're comfortable with. Here are the factors that determine your risk tolerance:

1. **Dependents Relying on You.** If you have people who depend on you financially, such as children or elderly family members, your risk tolerance should be lower. On the other hand, if you have no dependents, you can have more flexibility to take calculated risks.

2. **Age and Stage of Life.** Your age plays an important role in determining your risk tolerance. In general, younger investors can afford to take higher risks because they have a longer time horizon, allowing them to pursue investments with greater potential returns. Conversely, the closer you are to retirement, the more conservative your portfolio should be.

3. **Debt Situation.** Your debt situation significantly influences your risk tolerance. If you have substantial obligations, such as a mortgage or other loans, your risk tolerance is naturally lower, as your financial focus should be on managing and reducing these debts. Conversely, minimal or no debt increases your risk tolerance, allowing you to consider allocating more resources to higher-growth, riskier investments.

4. **Income Stability and Predictability.** The nature of your income—whether it's fixed and stable or variable and uncertain—should influence your risk tolerance. A steady paycheck provides a safety net, potentially allowing for a higher risk tolerance. On the other hand, if your income fluctuates or relies heavily on bonuses or commissions, a lower risk tolerance is advisable.

5. **Monthly Expenses.** A clear understanding of your fixed, variable, and contingency monthly expenses is essential. Fixed expenses are regular, non-negotiable costs such as rent, loan payments, or insurance premiums. Variable expenses, such as dining out, entertainment, or vacations, are less predictable but still need to be considered. Unforeseen expenses, like medical bills or home repairs, are unexpected costs that can further strain your finances if not accounted for. The lower your total monthly expenses (or estimated monthly expenses) across these categories, the greater your risk tolerance.

6. **Monthly Savings.** Your monthly savings, defined as the amount remaining after deducting expenses from your income, directly impacts your risk tolerance. A higher and consistent monthly savings rate increases your risk tolerance. On the other hand, minimal or irregular monthly savings reduce it.

7. **Future Inheritance.** Although it's a sensitive topic, discussing potential inheritances with your family can provide clarity about your long-term financial picture. Knowing you may receive a significant future inheritance increase your risk tolerance.

8. **Personal Comfort with Risk.** Finally, risk tolerance is highly personal. In addition to the factors outlined above, your comfort level with uncertainty and potential loss plays a critical role. Some people thrive on the excitement of higher risks and potential profits, while others prefer stability and predictability. Therefore, your risk tolerance—and by extension, your investment portfolio—should be evaluated not only based on the factors mentioned above but also on your personal sensitivity to risks and potential returns.

Cash Emergency Fund

Before you dive into creating a balanced investment portfolio, it's important to understand a fundamental concept: your cash emergency fund. This isn't just a financial buffer. It's your safety net, your peace of mind, and the foundation of a successful investing strategy. Without it, even the best investment plans can fall apart at the first sign of trouble. Your emergency fund is the amount of money you set aside in easily accessible savings to deal with unexpected events. Life is unpredictable, and surprises like medical bills, home repairs or job changes can happen when you least expect them. If you're forced to dip into your investments to cover these expenses, you risk selling at a loss or derailing your long-term financial goals. A well-structured emergency fund prevents this, allowing your investments to grow undisturbed while you deal with life's bumps in the road.

The size of your emergency fund depends on your risk tolerance, but most financial experts recommend covering your living expenses for a period of 3 to 12 months. However, I prefer a more conservative approach, so I recommend you maintaining an emergency fund that covers at least 6 months, and up to 24 months, of essential living expenses. To determine this, calculate your average monthly expenses.

Look at your bank statements from the past year, add up all your expenses, and divide the total by 12. This will give you a realistic figure for the monthly cost of your lifestyle. For example, if you spend $2,000 per month, your emergency fund should be between $12,000 (6 months) and $48,000 (24 months). The exact amount you choose depends on your risk tolerance, which, as we just discovered, is influenced by many factors such as age, job stability, family situation, and debt level.

Let's look at two examples at opposite ends of the spectrum. If you're very young, have no dependents, no significant financial obligations, and a stable income, a shorter emergency fund, around 6 months of expenses, might be sufficient. On the other hand, if you are at a more advanced stage of life, have children, a mortgage, and a variable income, a longer emergency fund of up to 24 months may offer the security you need. Depending on the factors we discussed earlier, your situation might align with one of these extremes or, more commonly, fall somewhere in between. Once you've calculated your emergency fund and, most importantly, ensured that this amount is available in your savings account, you'll be ready to allocate additional savings toward building an investment portfolio, engaging in short-term speculative activities, or both!

The Power of Compound Interest

Another fundamental concept every investor must understand is the extraordinary power of compound interest. Compound interest, often called the "eighth wonder of the world," is a cornerstone of wealth accumulation. It's the reason why starting to invest early, even with small amounts, can yield remarkable results over time. At its core, compounding on interest means earning interest not only on your initial investment, but also on the interest that accumulates over time. Unlike simple interest, which is calculated only on the principal amount, compound interest grows exponentially as your investment generates returns, and those returns generate more returns.

Before diving into an example, let's define two key terms: APR (Annual Percentage Rate) and APY (Annual Percentage Yield). APR is the nominal annual interest rate that does not account for the effects of compounding on interests. In contrast, APY reflects the actual growth of your investment by including the impact of compounding on interests. The more frequently compounding on interests occurs (e.g., annually, monthly, daily), the higher the APY compared to the APR.

Imagine you invest $1,000 at an interest rate of 8%, with interest compounded annually. Over the course of three years, here's how your investment grows under the APR model compared to the APY model:

Year 1

- APR growth: 8% of $1,000 = $80. The total is $1,080.

- APY growth: The total remains $1,080 in the first year because no previous interest has been compounded yet.

Year 2

- APR growth: Another 8% of the original $1,000 = $80, for a total of $1,160 (simple addition, ignoring compound interest).

- APY growth: Compound interest applies 8% to $1,080, not just the original $1,000. The new total is $1,166.40.

Year 3

- APR growth: Another 8% of $1,000 = $80, for a total of $1,240 (again, simple addition).

- APY growth: Compound interest applies 8% to $1,166.40. The new total becomes $1,259.71.

By the End of the Third Year

- The APR calculation shows a total growth of $240 ($80 × 3 years).

- The APY calculation shows a total growth of $259.71, thanks to compound interest.

This example demonstrates that compound interest, captured by APY, accelerates growth compared to the simpler APR model. The difference may seem small initially, but over time, compound interest creates a significant snowball effect, amplifying your returns dramatically. Compound interest is directly related to achieving financial independence and a comfortable retirement. The more time you give your money to grow, the less you'll need to save in later years to achieve the same goals. Starting young, even with modest monthly contributions, reduces the pressure to make large investments later in life, as these small, consistent contributions can snowball into substantial wealth over time.

Chapter 3: Exploring the Investment & Trading Landscape

The Stock Market Made Simple

Understanding the fundamentals of the stock market is critical because it's one of the most accessible and effective ways to build wealth. Let's break it down into its essential components and clarify what it all means. Stocks, also known as shares or equities, represent ownership in a company. When you buy a stock, you are buying a small piece of that company. Think of it as owning a piece of a large pie. This ownership entitles you to a share of the company's profits (if it chooses to distribute them) and possibly a say in some decisions through voting rights, although this is most relevant to large shareholders. When you buy a stock, you're investing in a company with the expectation that its value will increase over time. If the company performs well, its share price may rise, allowing you to sell your shares at a profit. On the other hand, if the company performs poorly, the stock price may fall, and you could lose money. Owning a stock is essentially betting on the future success of the company.

Dividends are a portion of a company's profits that it chooses to distribute to its shareholders. As mentioned, not all companies pay dividends; some prefer to reinvest their profits back into the business to fuel growth. For those that do, dividends can be an attractive feature, providing investors with a steady stream of income. For example, if you own 100 shares of a company that pays a dividend of $2 per share per year, you'd earn $200 in dividends. Dividend-paying stocks are often favored by income-oriented investors because they can generate passive income regardless of market fluctuations.

The stock market works on the principle of supply and demand. If more people want to buy a stock (demand) than want to sell it (supply), the price will rise. Conversely, when more people want to sell than buy, the price falls. This dynamic is influenced by a myriad of factors, including company performance, economic conditions, market sentiment, and global events. Stock exchanges are the marketplaces where stocks are bought and sold. They act as a bridge between buyers and sellers, ensuring transparency and fair pricing. Some well-known examples of exchanges include the New York Stock Exchange, the NASDAQ, and the London Stock Exchange. These exchanges provide the infrastructure for trading and set rules to ensure smooth operations. While most trading is now done digitally, exchanges remain crucial for maintaining market integrity and ensuring transparency.

To gauge the overall health of the stock market, investors often look at stock market indexes. These are benchmarks that track the performance of a group of stocks. Common examples include the S&P 500, which represents the 500 largest publicly traded companies in the United States, and the FTSE 100, which represents the 100 largest companies on the London Stock Exchange. Indexes are useful for assessing market trends and can also serve as investment vehicles through ETFs that replicate their performance, as we will discuss later.

What is Value Investing?

Value investing is one of the most talked about strategies in the financial world, based on the idea of buying stocks at a price below their intrinsic value. At its core, it's about identifying opportunities where the market has undervalued a stock based on its fundamentals, such as the company's earnings and growth potential. The philosophy behind value investing is simple: pay less than what something is worth, hold it for the long term, and let its true value eventually be reflected in the market price.

The strategy became famous through the work of Benjamin Graham[5], who introduced it as a foundational approach to investing, and Warren

---

[5] **Graham, B. (2006).** *The Intelligent Investor: The Definitive Book on Value Investing.* Revised Edition. Harper Business.

Buffett, who elevated it to legendary status. Value investing is based on the belief that markets are not always rational and that temporary mispricing of assets can create opportunities for savvy investors. The process typically involves analyzing financial statements, evaluating key metrics, and understanding the broader economic and market conditions affecting a company. The goal is to find companies that are fundamentally strong but currently undervalued due to market sentiment or temporary challenges. Once identified, the investor buys the stock and holds it until the market corrects its valuation.

While value investing is a powerful strategy, it doesn't fully align with the lazy investor philosophy outlined in this book. Its reliance on meticulous research and ongoing analysis requires a significant investment of time and effort. That said, this book is designed to make even complex strategies more accessible. In the following chapters, I'll walk you through a streamlined approach to value investing, covering the key metrics and providing a step-by-step strategy to help you identify undervalued stocks with confidence and ease. Once we've explored this, I'll introduce you to a much lazier, yet effective, alternative that aligns perfectly with our hands-off investment philosophy. Then, it will be up to you to decide whether to take on the long and detailed work of applying value investing yourself or to embrace the lazy alternative.

Building and Managing an Investment Portfolio: A First Look

Building an investment portfolio is the cornerstone of any long-term financial strategy. At its core, a portfolio is a collection of different investments chosen to match your financial goals, risk tolerance and investment horizon. Think of it as your personal wealth-building toolbox, with each asset serving a specific purpose to help you achieve financial stability and growth. Why is a portfolio important? Because it allows you to diversify. Diversification, that is spreading your investments across different types of assets, is one of the most effective ways to reduce risk while seeking consistent returns over time. Instead of putting all your eggs in one basket, a diversified portfolio ensures that even if one investment underperforms, others may perform well, balancing out the overall risk.

A portfolio can include a mix of assets such as stocks, ETFs, bonds, commodities, precious metals, and cryptocurrencies. Each of these assets has unique characteristics, levels of risk, and potential returns. In this book, we'll explore how to create a balanced portfolio specifically designed for the lazy investor, one that minimizes effort while maximizing long-term growth and success. We'll also look at strategies for managing and tweaking your portfolio over time to make sure it stays in line with your financial goals. For now, just remember: a well-constructed portfolio is your best ally in navigating the unpredictable world of investing and provides a solid foundation for achieving your long-term financial goals.

Day Trading: A First Look

Day trading represents a dramatic shift from the world of long-term investing, diving headfirst into the high-stakes realm of short-term speculation. Unlike traditional investing, where you buy assets with the intention of holding them for many years, day trading involves opening and closing positions within the same trading day. The goal? To capitalize on rapid price fluctuations in stocks, forex, cryptocurrencies, or other assets. It's not just a different game. It's an entirely different mindset. While a balanced investment portfolio focuses on gradual, steady wealth accumulation over time, day trading is about speed, precision, and a willingness to take significant risk for the chance of quick rewards. It's important to understand that these two financial activities, investing and day trading, are not mutually exclusive. You can have a long-term portfolio for wealth accumulation while exploring tools and strategies for short-term trading. However, it's important to treat them as separate activities, each with its own goals, strategies, and risk profiles. Day trading is inherently high risk and high potential reward. The potential for significant profits is alluring, but the reality is that the risks are equally, if not more, pronounced. It's not uncommon for traders to experience large losses if they are unprepared or overly emotional in their decision-making.

PART II: Value Investing and ETFs

Chapter 4: How to Pick Stocks Based on Value Investing

Categorizing Stocks

To truly grasp value investing, the first step is understanding the different categories of stocks. Stocks can be classified in various ways, each providing unique insights into their characteristics and potential. Here are the main classifications.

1. Market Capitalization

Stocks are often categorized based on the size of the company as measured by its market capitalization (market cap). This is calculated by multiplying the company's share price by the total number of shares outstanding. Market cap gives investors a sense of the company's size, growth potential and risk profile:

- **Large-cap stocks.** These are companies with a market capitalization of $10 billion or more. They tend to be well-established, financially stable, and less volatile.

- **Mid-cap stocks.** With market capitalizations between $2 billion and $10 billion, mid-cap companies often represent a balance between growth and stability. They may have more growth potential than large caps, but are riskier.

- **Small-cap stocks.** Companies with a market capitalization of less than $2 billion fall into this category. These stocks can offer significant growth opportunities, but come with higher risk and volatility.

2. Sector and Industry

Stocks are categorized not only by the sector but also by the specific industry within that sector in which the company operates. This classification helps investors diversify their portfolios across different areas of the economy, reducing risk if one sector or industry underperforms. Common sectors include:

- Technology
- Health Care
- Consumer Discretionary
- Financial Services
- Energy
- Utilities

Each sector may react differently to macroeconomic changes. For example, technology stocks can thrive during periods of innovation, while utilities tend to perform well during economic downturns. Within each sector, there are specific industries that provide even greater granularity. For example, within the Technology sector, common industries are Software, Semiconductors, and Hardware. Understanding these distinctions allows investors to make more informed decisions about diversification and risk management.

3. Growth vs. Value

Stocks can also be classified between growth and value stocks:

- **Growth stocks.** These are companies that are expected to grow their sales and earnings faster than the market average. They often reinvest their earnings to fuel expansion, which means they often don't pay dividends. While growth stocks can offer high returns, they're usually riskier and rarely meet the technical parameters for undervaluation that we will discuss later, because investors are willing to pay a premium for their expected future growth.

- **Value stocks.** These are companies that seem to be trading below their intrinsic value, making them potentially undervalued. Investors practicing value investing aim to identify these opportunities, focusing on stocks that offer strong fundamentals and long-term growth potential despite being overlooked and undervalued by the market.

4. <u>Common vs. Preferred</u>

Stocks can also be categorized based on the type of ownership they represent:

- **Common stocks.** These represent ownership in a company and usually come with voting rights. They are the most widely traded type of stock but offer no guaranteed dividends, unlike preferred stocks.

- **Preferred stock.** These shares have priority over common shares in the payment of dividends and the distribution of assets in the event of liquidation. They often offer fixed dividend payments and are less volatile, making them more attractive to income-oriented investors. However, they typically do not carry voting rights.

5. <u>Dividend vs. Non-Dividend</u>

Another way to classify stocks is by whether they pay dividends:

- **Dividend-paying stocks.** These stocks make regular payouts to shareholders, making them attractive to income-seeking investors. They are often large-cap, stable companies.

- **Non-dividend-paying stocks.** These are typically growth-oriented companies that reinvest earnings to expand operations. They appeal to investors more focused on capital appreciation.

6. <u>Cyclical vs. Defensive</u>

The behavior of stocks in response to economic cycles is another useful categorization:

- **Cyclical stocks.** These stocks are tied to the economic cycle and tend to perform well during periods of economic growth. Examples include automotive, luxury goods, and travel companies.

- **Defensive stocks.** These stocks are less affected by economic fluctuations and tend to perform consistently regardless of the economic climate. Examples include health care, utilities, and consumer staples.

7. Domestic vs. International

Finally, stocks can be categorized based on the geographic location of the company:

- **Domestic stocks.** These represent companies based in your home country, often offering familiarity and easier access to financial information.

- **International stocks.** These represent companies based in other countries, which can provide diversification and exposure to different economic conditions.

The 10 Principles of Value Investing

Here are the 10 key principles of value investing. Understanding these principles lays the foundation for effectively implementing value investing strategies.

1. Focus on Intrinsic Value

The cornerstone of value investing is the concept of intrinsic value (or fair value[6]), which represents a company's true worth, determined by its fundamentals, such as earnings and growth potential, rather than its current market price. Value investors seek to identify stocks that are trading at a discount to their intrinsic value.

---

[6] **Damodaran, A. (2012).** *Investment Valuation: Tools and Techniques for Determining the Value of Any Asset (3rd ed.).* Wiley.

2. Patience is Key

Value investing is by nature a long-term strategy. It requires the patience to hold investments for years, sometimes decades, while a company's intrinsic value is recognized by the market.

3. The Margin of Safety

One of the most important principles of value investing is to maintain a margin of safety, which represents the gap between a stock's intrinsic value and its current market price. This margin provides a cushion against valuation errors or unforeseen market downturns. For example, if a stock's intrinsic value is estimated to be $100 per share, a value investor might only consider buying it at $80 or less, ensuring a margin of safety of at least 20% to account for potential errors in valuation or unexpected market fluctuations.

4. Avoid Market Noise

Value investors consciously tune out market noise, which includes daily price fluctuations, sensational news, and overly optimistic or pessimistic forecasts. They focus on fundamentals rather than emotions, understanding that the stock market is not always rational in the short term, but tends to align with intrinsic value over the long term.

5. Focus on High-Quality Companies

Value investing isn't just about buying "cheap" stocks. It's about buying high-quality companies at a discount. These companies have strong financial health, consistent profitability, competitive advantages, and other attributes that we'll explore in detail later.

6. Diversification for Risk Management

While value investors seek to identify undervalued stocks, they also understand the importance of diversification. Spreading investments across different industries, sectors, and countries helps reduce the overall risk of a portfolio. Even the most carefully selected undervalued stocks can face unexpected challenges, making diversification essential.

7. Think Different

Value investors often go against the crowd, seeking opportunities in unloved or overlooked areas of the market. Stocks that have fallen out of favor due to temporary problems or negative sentiment can often present attractive opportunities. However, this requires a willingness to challenge conventional wisdom and confidence in one's research and analysis.

8. Discipline and Emotional Control

Market volatility can lead to fear during downturns and greed during rallies. Successful value investors remain disciplined and stick to their investment thesis even when others panic or chase trends. Emotional control is essential to making rational decisions and avoiding impulsive moves that can lead to losses.

9. Value Investing is Both a Science and an Art

Determining intrinsic value is both a science and an art. While value investors use quantitative methods, which we will explore shortly, they must also consider qualitative factors such as a company's competitive position, industry trends, and the quality of its management. Interpreting these elements requires a blend of analytical expertise and intuitive judgment.

10. Compounding Over Time

Value investing harnesses the power of compounding through dividends and long-term growth. Some stocks pay dividends, which investors can reinvest to purchase additional shares. This reinvestment creates a compounding effect, where dividends generate more dividends over time. By starting early and remaining consistent, even modest investments can grow significantly through the combined effects of reinvested dividends and the long-term appreciation of undervalued stocks.

Key Metrics to Identify Undervalued Stocks

Value investing relies heavily on the analysis of financial data to determine whether a stock is trading below its intrinsic value. While no single metric can provide a definitive answer, a combination of key metrics can provide a clearer picture of a company's true value. These tools are the foundation of value investing and help you determine whether a stock is undervalued. Here are the most important metrics and what they reveal.

1. Price-to-Earnings (P/E) Ratio

The P/E ratio is one of the most widely used valuation ratios. It compares a company's stock price per share to its earnings per share (EPS). EPS represents the portion of a company's profit allocated to each outstanding share of common stock, calculated by dividing the company's net income by the total number of outstanding shares. A low P/E ratio relative to industry peers or historical averages may indicate that the stock is undervalued. As a general rule, a P/E ratio below 15 can often be a starting point for identifying potentially undervalued stocks. However, this is not a hard-and-fast rule, as some sectors naturally have higher or lower average P/E ratios. Additionally, a low P/E ratio can sometimes signal problems, such as declining earnings or a lack of growth prospects, so understanding the context is critical.

- **Formula:** P/E ratio = Market price per share / Earnings per share.

- **Example:** If a company's stock is trading at $50 and its EPS is $5, the P/E ratio is 10. If similar companies in the industry have a P/E ratio of 20, the stock may be undervalued.

2. Earnings Yield

Earnings yield is the inverse of the P/E ratio and is expressed as a percentage. It indicates how much a company earns relative to its stock price, effectively showing the return an investor might expect if the company distributed all its profits as dividends. A high earnings yield relative to the market average or industry peers may suggest that a stock is undervalued. It is also a highly useful metric for comparing stocks to fixed-income investments, such as bonds.

- **Formula:** Earning Yield = Earnings per share / Market price per share.

- **Example:** A stock with an earnings yield of 8% may be more attractive than another stock in the same industry that has an earnings yield of 3%.

3. Price/Earnings-to-Growth (PEG) Ratio

The PEG ratio refines the P/E ratio by incorporating the company's expected growth rate. While the P/E ratio compares a company's stock price to its EPS, it doesn't account for how quickly those earnings are expected to grow. The PEG ratio adjusts for this by dividing the P/E ratio by the company's projected growth rate. This approach provides a more nuanced perspective on valuation by linking the price investors pay for earnings with how fast those earnings are expected to increase in the future. A PEG ratio of less than 1 is often seen as a potential signal of undervaluation, suggesting that the stock's price doesn't fully reflect its growth potential.

- **Formula:** PEG ratio = P/E ratio / annual EPS growth rate. Note: The annual EPS growth rate is expressed as a percentage but is used in the PEG formula as a whole number and not as a decimal.

- **Example:** A stock with a P/E ratio of 10 and an annual EPS growth rate of 15% has a PEG of 0.67, which may indicate undervaluation.

4. Price-to-Book (P/B) Ratio

The P/B ratio compares the market value of a company to its book value (assets minus liabilities). This ratio is particularly useful for evaluating asset-heavy industries, such as manufacturing. A P/B ratio below 1 could indicate undervaluation, but it's important to analyze the quality of the assets.

- **Formula:** P/B ratio = Market price per share / Book value per share.

- **Example:** If the P/B ratio is 0.8, the market is valuing the company at less than the net worth of its assets, which may signal a good buying opportunity.

5. Dividend Yield

The dividend yield is a metric that shows how much a company pays out in dividends each year relative to its share price. For companies that pay dividends, the dividend yield can indicate whether a stock is undervalued. A high yield relative to historical averages or industry benchmarks can indicate undervaluation, although it's important to ensure that the dividend is sustainable. As a general guideline, a dividend yield above 5% is often considered attractive for value investors. However, this is not a strict guideline, as certain sectors tend to have inherently higher or lower average dividend yields.

- **Formula:** Dividend Yield = Annual dividend per share / Market price per share.

- **Example:** If a stock pays $2 in annual dividends and trades at $40, the yield is 5%. If similar companies are yielding 3%, the stock may be undervalued.

6. Price-to-Free Cash Flow (P/FCF)

Free Cash Flow (FCF) represents the cash a company generates through its operations after accounting for capital expenditures (Capex). Capex refers to funds spent by a company to acquire or upgrade fixed, physical or non-consumable assets. In other words, Capex consists of investments in assets aimed at maintaining current operational levels and driving future growth. FCF shows whether a company has the capacity to reinvest in its business, pay dividends, reduce debt, or pursue growth opportunities. The P/FCF ratio compares a company's market price per share to its free cash flow per share. As a general guideline, a P/FCF ratio below 15 is often considered attractive for value investors. However, this benchmark can vary significantly across sectors and industries. Some industries naturally have higher P/FCF averages, while others may trend lower. Always compare a company's P/FCF ratio to its industry peers for a meaningful evaluation.

- **Formula 1:** FCF = Cash from operations – Capital expenditure (Capex).

- **Formula 2:** P / FCF = Market price per share / Free cash flow per share.

- **Example:** If a company's P/FCF is 12 and its industry peers average 18, the company may be undervalued.

7. <u>Return on Equity (ROE)</u>

Return on Equity (ROE) is a key profitability metric that shows how effectively a company uses its shareholders' equity to generate profits. Essentially, it measures the return investors receive for each dollar of equity they own. A high ROE indicates a company is efficiently utilizing its equity base to grow its business and create value for shareholders. As a general benchmark, a ROE above 20% is often considered strong for value investors. However, this figure can vary significantly depending on the sector and industry. A high ROE compared to industry averages, especially combined with a low P/E ratio, may indicate a high-quality, undervalued stock. However, it's important to ensure that the ROE is not artificially inflated by excessive debt, as this could signal higher risk.

- **Formula:** ROE = Net income / Shareholders' equity.

- **Example:** Suppose a company reports a net income of $10 million and has shareholders' equity of $50 million. This means the company generates a 20% return on the equity invested by its shareholders. If the industry average ROE is 15%, this company is outperforming its peers in effectively utilizing shareholder capital to generate profits.

8. Debt-to-Equity (D/E) Ratio

The debt-to-equity (D/E) ratio is an essential financial measure that highlights the balance between a company's borrowed funds (debt) and the capital provided by shareholders (equity). Essentially, it indicates the extent to which a company relies on debt versus equity to finance its operations and growth. D/E ratio is essential to understanding financial stability. Companies with high levels of debt relative to equity may struggle during economic downturns, making them riskier for value investors. As a general benchmark, a D/E ratio below 0.5 is often considered good. However, what qualifies as a "good" D/E ratio can vary by industry.

- **Formula:** D/E ratio = Total liabilities / Equity.

- **Example:** If a company has total liabilities of $500 million and shareholder equity of $1 billion, its D/E ratio would be 0.5. If this ratio is lower than the industry average, it may indicate a more stable financial position and a potentially lower-risk investment. Conversely, if the ratio is significantly higher than the industry average, it could suggest that the company is more reliant on debt, making it a riskier investment, especially in volatile market conditions.

9. Current Ratio and Quick Ratio

These two metrics measure a company's short-term liquidity, or its ability to meet short-term obligations with its current assets. Both are essential for evaluating financial stability, especially in industries where liquidity is critical. Companies with low liquidity ratios may struggle to meet short-term obligations, whereas excessively high ratios might indicate poor asset management. Both indicators are best used in conjunction with others, such as the debt-to-equity ratio, to form a holistic view of financial stability.

Current Ratio: The current ratio compares a company's total current assets to its total current liabilities. It shows whether the company can cover its short-term debts using assets that are expected to be converted into cash within a year. A current ratio above 1.2 typically indicates strong liquidity, suggesting that the company has sufficient current assets to cover its current liabilities. However, an excessively high current ratio (above 3) might indicate inefficiency in utilizing assets.

Formula: Current ratio = Current assets / Current liabilities.

Quick Ratio: The quick ratio is a stricter measure of liquidity compared to the current ratio. It excludes inventory and other less-liquid current assets from the calculation, focusing only on highly liquid assets like cash, marketable securities, and accounts receivable. A quick ratio above 1.1 indicates that the company can cover its short-term liabilities without relying on inventory sales. This is particularly important for companies in industries where inventory may take time to convert into cash. However, an excessively high quick ratio (above 3) might indicate inefficiency in utilizing assets.

Formula: Quick ratio = (Current assets - inventory) / Current liabilities.

Example: Suppose a company has:

- Current assets of $200,000.
- Inventory worth $50,000.
- Current liabilities of $100,000.
- Current Ratio: $200,000 / $100,000 = 2.0.
- Quick Ratio: ($200,000 - $50,000) / $100,000 = 1.5.

Step by Step Process for Successful Value Investing

In this section, we'll take the metrics we've just explored and apply them within a practical, step-by-step process to help you identify and purchase undervalued stocks. By following these steps, you'll be equipped to move confidently from theoretical analysis to actionable investment decisions.

1. Begin Your Search with a Stock Screener

Begin by using a stock screener, a powerful tool that allows you to filter and sort stocks based on various criteria. As a personal recommendation, my favorite is Finviz.com, because of its highly customizable filters. However, feel free to explore other stock screeners and choose the one that best fits your needs. Once you access the tool, the first step is to apply filters to define the pool of stocks you want to analyze. Start with 5 parameters:

- **Country.** Select the country where the companies operate.

- **Sector.** Choose the sector of interest (e.g., Industrials, Technology).

- **Industry.** Narrow it further by selecting a specific industry within the sector (e.g., Computer Hardware within Technology).

- **Market Capitalization > $2 Billion.** Focus on companies with a market cap above this threshold to prioritize more stable and established firms. Smaller companies can offer high growth potential, but they are typically more volatile and carry higher risks, making them less suitable for long-term value investors.

- **P/E ratio < 15.** Apply this key metric for your initial screening. It's a powerful filter to generate preliminary hypotheses (to be further validated) about companies that may be potentially undervalued.

Applying these filters will yield very few results. Take the time to repeat this process across multiple industries within the country and sector you've chosen. Take note of every stock that passes this first screening. These are your initial candidates for deeper analysis in the next step. Note: P/E ratio less than 15 is a general benchmark value, but as previously mentioned, it varies significantly depending on the sector, country, and even the industry within the sector. If you notice that you're analyzing a sector where the average P/E is higher or lower than 15, adjust your filter accordingly by raising or lowering the threshold to align with the specific context.

2. Compare Key Metrics to Industry Averages

Now that you've identified potential candidates, it's time to take your analysis to the next level. Start by removing the P/E filter while keeping the other previously applied filters active. For each company that passed the initial P/E screening, adjust the industry filter to align with the specific sector of the company you're analyzing. Then, compare the following metrics against the corresponding industry averages. Specifically:

- **PEG Ratio.** As discussed earlier, the PEG ratio combines a company's P/E ratio with its projected earnings growth rate. The PEG ratio found in stock screeners like Finviz is typically calculated by considering both historical growth trends and analysts' forecasts of future earnings potential. As a general rule, a PEG ratio below 1 may indicate that the stock is undervalued relative to its growth potential. However, compare this value to the industry average for a more accurate assessment. The lower the PEG ratio compared to peers, the better.

- **P/B Ratio.** A P/B ratio below 1 is generally considered good, as it may indicate the company is undervalued relative to its book value. However, always compare this value to the industry average. A P/B lower than the industry average may indicate the stock is undervalued.

- **Dividend Yield.** If the company distributes dividends, this can be an added benefit, but it's important not to base your decision solely on dividend payments, as capital gains also contribute to your returns. As a broad guideline, a dividend yield above 5% may suggest potential undervaluation. However, it's crucial to compare this yield against the industry average.

- **P/FCF.** While a general benchmark suggests that a P/FCF ratio below 15 may indicate the stock is undervalued, it's very important to compare this ratio with the industry average. The lower the ratio compared to peers, the better.

- **ROE.** A general benchmark suggests that a ROE above 20% is desirable. However, focus more on how the company's ROE

45

compares to the industry average. A higher ROE relative to peers typically indicates more efficient use of equity.

- **D/E Ratio.** While a D/E ratio below 0.5 is often considered a sign of financial stability, it's essential to evaluate it within the context of the industry. Compare the company's D/E ratio to the industry average: a lower ratio indicates lower risk and greater financial resilience.

- **Current Ratio.** A ratio between 1.2 and 3 is generally considered healthy, indicating the company can meet its short-term obligations. As usual, always verify how this compares to the industry average.

- **Quick Ratio.** Similar to the current ratio, a quick ratio between 1.1 and 3 is usually seen as solid. Again, prioritize companies with ratios in this range that also outperform their industry peers.

You can determine the industry averages for these metrics directly within the stock screener by manually reviewing all the stocks in the industry. To ensure more precise and meaningful results, keep the filters for sector, industry, market cap, and country active. Sort the results by the specific metric to compare, and review the stocks that appear in the filtered list. Alternatively, you can search for industry-specific reports available on financial websites.

Keep in mind that you're unlikely to find a stock where all these indicators are better than the industry average. The key is to evaluate each stock holistically and determine which one exhibits the strongest overall performance across the metrics. Based on this assessment, select the stock that you believe has the most potential due to its superior alignment with value investing principles. This company will move forward to the next step in the process.

3. <u>Deep Dive into the Company's Financials</u>

Once you've identified a standout company from your initial screening and metric comparisons, it's time to delve deeper into its financial health. Download the company's financial statements directly from its website, typically found in the Investor Relations section. These documents include the Income Statement, Balance Sheet, and Cash Flow Statement, providing the most reliable and comprehensive view of the company's financial health.

1. **Income Statement.** Check for steady growth in revenues and profits over the past five years. A company with consistently increasing revenues demonstrates strong demand for its products or services, while growing earnings indicate efficient operations and profitability.

2. **Balance Sheet.** Evaluate the company's total assets, liabilities, and equity. Pay attention to liquidity by examining again the current ratio and the quick ratio. Additionally, while we've already considered the D/E ratio earlier, revisit it here with a closer lens. Be cautious with companies heavily reliant on debt, especially in sectors prone to economic cycles.

3. **Cash Flow Statement.** This document reveals the actual cash generated and used by the company. Focus on Free Cash Flows (FCFs), which we discussed earlier. Consistent and growing FCFs over the past five years indicate that the company is effectively generating cash to sustain its operations, reinvest in growth, and potentially pay dividends (or start paying them in the future). Conversely, declining FCFs may signal financial difficulties or operational inefficiencies.

For beginners, financial statements may seem intimidating. If you're new to analyzing financial statements, you can rely on online platforms that offer simplified summaries and expert analyses to help make the data more accessible and easier to interpret. If the company has also successfully passed this analysis, you can move on to the next step.

4. <u>Conduct the Qualitative Analysis</u>

Numbers only tell part of the story; qualitative factors are equally critical when evaluating a stock. These elements provide deeper insight into the company's long-term viability and growth potential. Here's how to perform a thorough qualitative analysis for the company selected:

- **Understand the Business Model.** Investigate how the company generates revenue. What distinguishes it from its competitors? Does it have a unique value proposition, and what is its position within the industry? A strong business model should be straightforward to understand and show resilience across market conditions.

- **Assess Competitive Advantage.** Identify whether the company has a sustainable competitive advantage, often referred to as an "economic moat". This could include factors like a strong brand, proprietary technology, patents, cost leadership, or a dominant market share. Companies with durable competitive advantages are better positioned for long-term success.

- **Evaluate Future Risks.** Examine the company's reports and industry outlook. Are there emerging risks, such as regulatory challenges or changing consumer preferences, that could impact future performance?

- **Consider Its Maturity Phase.** Is the company in a high-growth phase with significant potential (but higher risk), or is it a mature business offering stability with limited growth? Knowing where the company stands in its life cycle can help you align your investment with your risk tolerance and goals.

- **Analyze Management Quality.** Research the management team's experience and track record. Are they known for delivering results and creating shareholder value? Platforms like Glassdoor can provide employee feedback on leadership effectiveness. Strong management is often a key driver of a company's success.

- **Assess Price Proximity to All-Time Highs.** Consider how the stock's current price compares to its historical highs and lows. Clearly, stocks trading at or near all-time highs are less attractive.

- **Gauge Customer Satisfaction.** Look for customer feedback online. Satisfied customers can be a good indicator of a company's brand loyalty and product or service quality. Conversely, consistent complaints could signal potential issues.

- **Evaluate the Impact of Macroeconomic Cycles.** Evaluate how broader economic trends and cycles might affect the company's performance. Does the company demonstrate resilience during economic downturns, or is its success heavily reliant on periods of economic growth?

As with the quantitative factors discussed earlier, it's important to recognize, once again, that no company will tick every box perfectly. Every business has its flaws and inherent risks. The key is to take a holistic view, considering how the company performs across various factors to determine if it is fundamentally strong and a worthwhile investment. If your analysis suggests that the company has solid strengths across multiple qualitative factors, and any weaknesses seem manageable or non-critical, you can move forward to the next phase of your evaluation. However, if significant risks or red flags emerge during this step, it may be wise to abandon the investment idea and focus your efforts elsewhere.

5. Conduct Discounted Cash Flow (DCF) Analysis

When you buy a stock, you are essentially purchasing a contract or ownership stake capable of generating cash flows in the future. The Discounted Cash Flow (DCF) analysis allows you to estimate the present value of these future cash flows. As Warren Buffett famously said, "Intrinsic value is the discounted value of the cash that can be taken out of a business during its remaining life[7]". The DCF method calculates this value by forecasting future cash flows and discounting them back to their present value. Here's the step-by-step process:

---

[7] **Buffett, W. (2019).** *The Essays of Warren Buffett: Lessons for Corporate America.* Edited by Lawrence A. Cunningham, 5th ed., Wiley, 2019.

5.1. Estimate Future Cash Flows

Future cash flow estimation involves projecting a company's net cash inflows over a specific period, typically five years. To begin, calculate the company's historical cash flow growth rate. You can find this data directly in the company's financial statements or through general financial platforms that aggregate such information. Take the cash flow figures from the last five years and determine the average annual growth rate. This gives you a starting point for projecting future cash flows. However, these projections should not rely solely on historical trends; they must also incorporate your qualitative and quantitative analysis from previous steps. Factors like the company's competitive position, management quality, and macroeconomic conditions may influence its ability to sustain or exceed historical growth rates.

Let's take as an example a company with the same name as my community, "Crypto Go". Let's say Crypto Go reported $100 million in cash flow in its most recent financial statement, and five years ago, it reported $88.9 million. This represents a total growth of approximately 12.5% over five years, or an average annual growth rate of 2.5%. However, based on your analysis of industry conditions, you decide to be conservative and project a future annual growth rate of 2%. Using this rate, the estimated cash flows for the next five years are as follows:

- Year 1: $100M \times (1 + 0.02) = $102 M.
- Year 2: $102M \times (1 + 0.02) = $104.04 M.
- Year 3: $104.04M \times (1 + 0.02) = $106.12 M.
- Year 4: $106.12M \times (1 + 0.02) = $108.24 M.
- Year 5: $108.24M \times (1 + 0.02) = $110.41 M.

The projected cash flows for each of the next five years are now calculated. These projections serve as the basis for further steps in the DCF analysis, where they will be discounted to their present value using a discount rate.

5.2. Discount Future Cash Flows to the Present Day

The future value of money is not equal to its present value due to inflation and opportunity costs. Therefore, future cash flows need to be "discounted" back to their present value using a discount rate. This adjustment reflects the principle that a dollar today is worth more than a dollar in the future. A commonly used discount rate is 10%, which corresponds to the historical average long-term return of the S&P 500[8]. Alternatively, a more tailored rate can be calculated by combining two key components:

- **Risk-Free Rate.** This is typically the yield on government bonds, as they are generally considered low-risk investments.

- **Risk Premium.** This accounts for the specific risks associated with the company or the industry in question, adding a percentage to the risk-free rate to reflect these uncertainties.

Many investors, including myself, prefer simplicity and use a fixed rate of 10% as a general benchmark for discounting. However, you can adjust this rate based on your own analysis and the specific characteristics of the company being evaluated.

To calculate the discounted cash flows for each year, the formula is:

$$\text{Discounted Cash Flow} = \frac{\text{Cash Flow}}{(1 + \text{Discount Rate})^n}$$

Where n is the number of the year. To calculate the total discounted cash flows for five years, the formula becomes:

$$\text{Total Discounted Cash Flows} = \frac{CF_1}{(1+DR)^1} + \frac{CF_2}{(1+DR)^2} + \frac{CF_3}{(1+DR)^3} + \frac{CF_4}{(1+DR)^4} + \frac{CF_5}{(1+DR)^5}$$

---

[8] **Malkiel, B. G. (2020).** *A Random Walk Down Wall Street: The Time-Tested Strategy for Successful Investing.* W.W. Norton & Company.

Returning to our example of the company "Crypto Go", assuming a discount rate of 10%, the discounted cash flows for each year would be:

$$\text{Year 1: } \frac{102}{(1+0.10)^1} = 92.73M$$

$$\text{Year 2: } \frac{104.04}{(1+0.10)^2} = 85.92M$$

$$\text{Year 3: } \frac{106.12}{(1+0.10)^3} = 79.64M$$

$$\text{Year 4: } \frac{108.24}{(1+0.10)^4} = 73.85M$$

$$\text{Year 5: } \frac{110.41}{(1+0.10)^5} = 68.43M$$

Summing these up gives the total discounted cash flows over five years:

Total = 92.73 + 85.92 + 79.64 + 73.85 + 68.43 = $400.57 M.

This total represents the present value of the company's projected cash flows over the next five years. In the next step, we'll calculate the terminal value.

5.3. Calculate the Terminal Value and Discounted Terminal Value

The terminal value represents the value of all future cash flows a company is expected to generate beyond the forecasted period (in our example, 5 years), assuming it continues operating indefinitely. It's essentially a symbolic figure based on the theoretical scenario where the company survives forever. To calculate this, we use the "infinite growth rate", which reflects the annual growth rate of the company's cash flows into perpetuity. A common reference is the average global GDP growth rate, which is approximately 3%[9]. Adjustments are made based on the type of company:

- 2% for mature, slow-growing companies.
- 3% for most firms, aligning with average global GDP growth.

---

[9] **Damodaran, A. (2012).** *Investment Valuation: Tools and Techniques for Determining the Value of Any Asset (3rd ed.).* Wiley.

- 4% for fast-growing companies.

The formula for calculating terminal value is as follows:

$$TV = (CF_s \times (1 + IG)) / (DR - IG)$$

Where:

- CF_s = Cash flow in the final year of our forecast (Year 5 in our example).
- DR = Discount rate.
- IG = Infinite growth rate.

Let's return to our example of Crypto Go. Our cash flow in Year 5 is $110.41 M, the discount rate (DR) is 10%, ant the infinite growth rate (IG) is 3%.

Using the formula:

- Terminal Value (TV) = $(110.41 \times (1 + 0.03)) / (0.10 - 0.03)$ = $1,624.60 M.

Once the terminal value is calculated, it must be discounted to its present value using the same formula from Step 5.2. This ensures consistency in aligning all cash flow values to the present day. The discounting must use the last period selected for calculating our future cash flows—in our example, 5 years. The formula is:

- Discounted $TV = TV / (1 + DR)^5$

In our example:

- Discounted $TV = 1,624.60 / (1 + 0.10)^5$ = $1,008.75 M.

5.4. Calculate Intrinsic Value and Intrinsic Value per Share

Finally, to determine the intrinsic value (IV) of the company, the formula is the following:

- IV = Sum of Discounted Cash Flows + Discounted Terminal Value + Total Cash & Cash Equivalents

We've already calculated the first two components of this formula. The final component, total cash & cash equivalents, refers to the liquid assets a company holds, including money in bank accounts and highly liquid investments that can be quickly converted into cash. This information is readily available on the company's balance sheet. For our example, let's assume that Crypto Go currently holds $150 million in total cash & cash equivalents. Therefore, in our example:

- Sum of discounted cash flows: $400.57 M.
- Discounted terminal value: $1,008.75 M.
- Total cash & cash equivalents: $150 M.
- IV = 1,008.75 + 400.57 + 150.00 = $1,559.32 M.

To convert the intrinsic value into a per-share figure, divide the total intrinsic value by the number of outstanding shares. Supposing Crypto Go has 500 million outstanding shares:

- Intrinsic Value per Share = IV / Outstanding Shares = $1,559.32 / 500 = $3.12 per share.

5.5. Compare Intrinsic Value per Share with Market Price and Apply a Margin of Safety

The final step is to compare the intrinsic value per share with the current market price of the stock. Here's how to interpret the results:

- If the intrinsic value per share is higher than the market price, the stock is undervalued by the market.

- If the intrinsic value per share is lower than the market price, the stock is overvalued by the market.

- If the intrinsic value per share is approximately equal to the market price, the stock is fairly valued by the market.

Even if a stock appears undervalued, it's crucial to incorporate a margin of safety to account for uncertainties, potential errors in your assumptions, or unforeseen events. This margin acts as a protective buffer, reducing the risk of losses if the market price diverges from your valuation. Personally, I prefer a minimum margin of safety of 15%. While meeting the margin of safety threshold is essential, a market price far below the intrinsic value per share presents an even better opportunity. The lower the market price is compared to the intrinsic value, the greater the potential upside.

In our example, the intrinsic value per share for Crypto Go was determined to be $3.12. Applying a 15% margin of safety, you would only consider buying the stock if its market price is: $3.12 - (15% of $3.12) = $2.65 or lower.

In this case:

- If the market price of Crypto Go is $1.50, it would be a compelling opportunity, as it is significantly below your margin of safety threshold.

- If the market price is $2.80, it is borderline, but you might consider other factors like qualitative analysis before deciding.

- If the market price is $4.50, the stock is overvalued, and you should avoid it.

Note: While DCF analysis is highly effective for most industries, it is not the most suitable approach for valuing banks and other financial institutions due to the unique nature and complexity of their cash flows.

6. Consult News and Expert Analyses

Once you've formed your own assessment of the company, it's time to broaden your perspective by consulting external analyses and reviewing recent news. This step ensures you're not missing critical information and allows you to compare your evaluation with those of professional experts. Focus on the following:

Analyst Reports. Look for independent analyst evaluations of the company. These reports can provide valuable insights, particularly if there's a strong consensus among analysts with "buy" ratings and price targets at least 20% higher than the current market price. While many tools offer this data, two stand out:

- Yahoo Finance. A user-friendly platform that aggregates analyst opinions, including average price targets and ratings.

- Simply Wall Street. A premium tool offering in-depth analyses of nearly every stock worldwide, providing detailed metrics and intuitive data presentations.

News. Investigate recent news and developments related to the company. This step is crucial to uncover any events or issues that may impact its future performance. Reliable sources for news include the Wall Street Journal, Bloomberg, CNBC, Financial Times, and Yahoo Finance.

By consulting these resources, you can validate your findings, refine your analysis, and ensure no major risks or opportunities have been overlooked.

7. Plan Your Entry

Once you've identified a stock that aligns with your value investing criteria, the next step is deciding how to enter the position. You can choose between two alternative approaches:

- **Dollar-Cost Averaging (DCA).** With DCA, you invest a fixed amount of money at regular intervals, regardless of the stock's price. For instance, if you plan to invest $5,000, you could spread this amount over five months, investing $1,000 each month. This strategy reduces the impact of short-term price volatility and lowers the risk of buying at a peak.

- **Full Investment Upfront.** If your analysis strongly indicates that the stock is significantly undervalued, you may opt to invest the entire amount at once. This strategy allows you to take immediate advantage of the stock's low price and maximize potential gains if the price rises as expected. However, it carries greater risk, as the stock price could drop further after your purchase.

8. Plan Your Exit

As you might expect, the most natural exit strategy for a value investor is to sell the stock when its market price approaches (or closely matches) the intrinsic value per share you calculated. At that point, the stock is no longer undervalued, and the opportunity for further gains may be limited. However, it's essential to recognize that the intrinsic value you initially calculated isn't set in stone. The company's financial health, growth prospects, and other factors can change over time, impacting its intrinsic value. Therefore, it is wise to revisit your analysis periodically—every six months, for instance—to evaluate whether any significant changes have occurred that could impact your calculation of intrinsic value. If the fundamentals deteriorate or unexpected negative news emerges, you may need to adjust your intrinsic value downward and reconsider your position. Conversely, positive developments may justify an upward revision.

Macroeconomic changes can also influence your exit strategy. For instance, shifts in interest rates, consumer demand, or industry trends may alter the company's prospects and, consequently, its intrinsic value. Monitoring the broader economic landscape and its potential impact on your investment is just as crucial as analyzing the company itself. Finally, a partial exit can also align with portfolio rebalancing, a crucial aspect of any long-term investment strategy. This ensures your portfolio remains diversified and aligned with your goals. We'll delve deeper into rebalancing and other portfolio management strategies in later chapters, including how many stocks you should ideally hold for proper diversification.

Chapter 5: Why Value Investing (Often) Sucks for Lazy Investors

Congratulations on making it this far! You've just tackled one of the most challenging parts of this book: the chapter on value investing. If any part of it feels unclear, take your time to revisit the concepts, digest the information, and deepen your understanding. It's perfectly normal to feel overwhelmed. Value investing can be daunting, especially for beginners. This chapter, by contrast, is simpler and faster to absorb. The deliberately provocative title is meant to highlight that conducting the type of in-depth value investing analysis we explored in Chapter 4 isn't suited for everyone; and particularly not for lazy investors, which you might identify as. The reasons why value investing might not be ideal for a lazy investor are outlined in the next two concise subchapters. Let's dive in.

The Myth of Beating the Market Consistently

The allure of "beating the market" captures the imagination of many investors. In simple terms, beating the market means achieving investment returns that exceed the average performance of a major stock market index, such as the S&P 500 in the United States or similar benchmarks around the world. For example, if a market index grows by 8% in a year, an investor who achieves a 10% return is said to have beaten the market. Who wouldn't want to outperform the broader market and leave the average investor in the dust? The reality, however, paints a very different picture. The data is clear: consistently beating the market over the long term is extraordinarily rare, even for the most experienced professionals.

Let's take the example of actively managed funds in the United States, where detailed data is readily available. According to available reports, 94% of actively managed funds underperform the S&P 500 over a 20-

year period[10]. Even over shorter periods, such as 5 or 10 years, the numbers are not much better. If professional fund managers with teams of analysts, cutting-edge technology, and significant financial resources are struggling to beat the market, what are the odds for an individual investor? Even legendary investors often say that their level of success is not easily replicated. For example, Warren Buffett has suggested that most people are better off investing in ETFs (that we will discuss in the next chapter) than trying to pick individual stocks[11], emphasizing that the simplicity of copying the market often beats the complexity of trying to outsmart it.

This doesn't mean it's impossible for you to beat the market, especially if you carefully follow the strategies outlined in Chapter 4, where we explored value investing in detail. With discipline, thorough research, and the right approach, it's certainly achievable. However, as the data suggests, consistently outperforming the market is an uphill battle, even for seasoned professionals. As we'll see in the next chapter, adopting a market-matching strategy doesn't mean settling for mediocrity. On the contrary, it's a smart and strategic way to build wealth over time while avoiding the pitfalls and stress associated with active investing. The myth of beating the market consistently is the first reason why value investing often sucks for a lazy investor. Let's dive into the second reason.

Effort, Time and...Passion!

The second, and perhaps equally obvious, reason why value investing often sucks for lazy investors is the effort and time it requires. By now, after going through Chapter 4, you've likely realized just how demanding this approach can be. Conducting detailed analyses, calculating intrinsic values, and examining a company's fundamentals isn't exactly a walk in the park. And it doesn't stop there. You'll need to repeat these

---

[10] **S&P Dow Jones Indices (2021).** *SPIVA U.S.* Year-End 2021: Scorecard.

[11] **Buffett, W. (2016).** *Berkshire Hathaway Annual Shareholder Letter.*

analyses regularly, at least once every six months, to ensure the factors influencing your valuation haven't changed. On top of that, staying constantly informed is essential. You'll need to keep up with financial news, track global and domestic economic developments, monitor updates about the companies in your portfolio, and watch for any red flags or opportunities. Not exactly the dream setup for a very lazy investor.

But what does all this have to do with passion? After focusing so much on numbers and analysis, let's take a moment for something more personal and emotional. Passion is a crucial factor in determining whether value investing is right for you. If you genuinely enjoy diving into financial statements, analyzing business fundamentals, forming a long-term connection with the companies in your portfolio, and staying informed about financial markets, value investing could be an excellent fit—and even a rewarding part of your life. However, if these activities don't excite you, the time and effort required for value investing might quickly become overwhelming. Ultimately, a lack of time or effort often stems from one thing: a lack of passion. When you're passionate about something, you make it a priority, find time for it, and embrace the challenges as part of the experience. Without that intrinsic motivation, value investing can feel burdensome—far from the relaxed, low-effort approach that aligns with a lazy investor's philosophy.

If value investing doesn't align with your interests, there's no need to force it. The good news is there's a simpler, more accessible option that perfectly suits a lazy investor's mindset: ETFs. In the next chapter, we'll explore how ETFs can simplify investing while still delivering strong returns.

Chapter 6: The Power of ETFs

What are ETFs?

An Exchange-Traded Fund (ETF) is essentially a basket of investments, such as stocks, bonds, commodities, or other assets, packaged into a single security that trades on an exchange. Think of it as buying a whole range of investments in one convenient package. One of the biggest benefits of ETFs is diversification. When you buy an ETF, you're investing in a collection of assets rather than a single one. For example, an ETF that tracks the S&P 500 index gives you exposure to 500 of the largest companies in the market. This diversification spreads your risk. If one company underperforms, its impact on the overall ETF is minimized by the performance of the other assets in the basket.

ETFs are also notable for their low cost. ETFs are passively managed, meaning they aim to replicate the performance of an index rather than relying on expensive fund managers to select individual assets. This simplicity translates into lower fees, often as low as 0.03% to 0.4% annually, compared with the 1% to 2% charged by actively managed mutual funds[12]. Over time, these fee savings can add up significantly, making ETFs a more efficient way to build wealth, especially considering that, as we discussed earlier, 94% of active funds fail to outperform the market. So why not choose a low-cost tool that directly replicates market performance, effectively outperforming 94% of active funds, while also saving you money on fees?

Another standout feature of ETFs is their high liquidity, allowing investors to buy and sell them easily during market hours. Additionally, ETFs are remarkably transparent, with most providing daily disclosure

---

[12] **Vanguard Group. (2022).** *The Case for Index-Fund Investing.* Vanguard Research.

of their holdings. This clarity offers investors a unique level of visibility into where their money is allocated, which is uncommon in the financial world.

Different Types of ETFs

ETFs come in a wide range of options, each designed to replicate the performance of different underlying assets. Below are some of the most common types of ETFs:

Equity ETFs

The largest portion of your portfolio should consist of equity ETFs. Why? Historically, no asset class has outperformed equities when it comes to wealth creation. Private enterprise is the engine of innovation, development, and prosperity in a capitalist society, making equity the most important component of any long-term investment strategy.

Equity ETFs can be categorized in several ways:

- **By Region.** ETFs that track specific continents or global areas, such as World, North America, Europe, or emerging markets.

- **By Country.** ETFs that focus on specific countries, such as the United States, Japan, or Germany.

- **By Sector.** ETFs that specialize in industries like technology, healthcare, or energy.

- **By Theme.** ETFs centered around specific themes, such as circular economy, AI, or cybersecurity.

- **By Strategy.** ETFs targeting certain equity attributes, such as market capitalization (large, mid, or small caps), volatility, dividends, or fundamental metrics.

Bond ETFs

Bond ETFs represent another significant category, designed to replicate the performance of different types of bonds. These are ideal for balancing risk in your portfolio.

Bond ETFs can be categorized in several ways:

- **By Region or Country.** ETFs focusing on bonds from specific geographic regions or individual countries.

- **By Type of Bond.** Bond ETFs can specialize in certain types of bonds, such as government bonds, corporate bonds, or a combination of both (known as aggregate bond ETFs).

- **By Maturity.** Bond ETFs can be grouped by the maturity of their underlying bonds.

- **By Bond Rating.** Bond ETFs can be grouped by the rating of their underlying bonds, for example AAA rating.

Commodity ETFs

Commodity ETFs provide exposure to physical assets without requiring you to own them directly. These ETFs can include:

- **Precious Metals.** ETFs focused on assets like gold, silver, or platinum.

- **Commodity Segments.** ETFs that track a basket of multiple commodities within specific segments, such as agriculture or energy.

- **Single Commodities.** ETFs tracking specific commodities like oil, natural gas, or coffee.

Cryptocurrency ETFs

While cryptocurrency ETFs are gaining popularity, I don't recommend them. Investing in cryptocurrencies through ETFs goes against the fundamental principles of cryptocurrencies, such as decentralization and direct ownership. For a deeper exploration of this perspective, I encourage you to read my book, *"Cryptocurrency Investing"*.

Real Estate ETFs

Real estate ETFs provide investors with exposure to the property market without the need to own physical assets. These ETFs may focus on real estate investment trusts (REITs), which own and manage income-generating properties, or they can include broader real estate-related assets such as property development companies and real estate services firms. Also, these ETFs can target specific regions or countries. They are an effective way to gain access to the property sector in a convenient and liquid format.

Smart Beta ETFs

Smart Beta ETFs occupy a distinct niche within the ETF landscape, combining aspects of both passive and active investing. Unlike traditional ETFs that simply track an index, Smart Beta ETFs use pre-defined rules to select and weight their holdings based on specific factors such as valuation metrics, volatility, dividend yields, or other financial indicators. These criteria govern not only which companies are included in the ETF but also when they are added or removed.

For instance, a Smart Beta ETF focused on dividend yields might consist of companies with a history of consistently high dividend payouts, while removing those that no longer meet a specific threshold. Similarly, a Smart Beta ETF targeting low volatility would adjust its holdings to prioritize companies with historically stable stock price movements. These ETFs are particularly attractive to investors seeking targeted exposure to specific investment factors or strategies, offering a structured and systematic approach without the hands-on involvement and higher costs associated with actively managed funds.

Key Features of ETFs

Before investing in an ETF, it's crucial to understand its key features. Here's a brief overview of what to consider:

1. Naming

ETFs names may seem complex at first glance, but they are structured to convey important details about them. Let's break down an example: iShares Core S&P 500 UCITS ETF USD (Acc).

- **iShares.** This indicates the provider or issuer of the ETF. In this case, iShares, a division of BlackRock, is one of the largest and most reputable ETF providers globally.

- **Core.** This suggests that the ETF is designed to serve as the foundation of a long-term investment portfolio. Core ETFs often have lower fees and broad market exposure, making them ideal for a diversified portfolio.

- **S&P 500.** This specifies the index that the ETF tracks. In this case, it replicates the performance of the S&P 500, an index composed of 500 large-cap U.S. companies.

- **UCITS.** This stands for Undertakings for Collective Investment in Transferable Securities, a European regulatory framework. UCITS ETFs are highly regulated and offer great investor protections, making them popular among European investors.

- **ETF.** This simply indicates that the investment product is an Exchange-Traded Fund.

- **USD.** This specifies the fund's currency, meaning the currency in which the ETF calculates its net asset value and conducts its internal operations. Note that this may differ from the trading currency used on exchanges. In this case, the fund currency is USD.

- **Acc.** This means the ETF is an accumulating ETF, where dividends are automatically reinvested into the fund rather than paid out to investors. If it were a distributing fund, it would be marked as "Dist", indicating that dividends are distributed to investors.

2. Size

The size of an ETF refers to the total amount of money invested in it and serves as a useful indicator of its popularity. While larger ETFs managing billions of dollars are often associated with higher liquidity, this isn't always the case. The liquidity of an ETF is primarily determined by the liquidity of its underlying assets, rather than its size.

Therefore, even small ETFs can offer sufficient liquidity for everyday trading.

3. Costs

ETFs are widely appreciated for their low costs, but even within the ETF landscape, fees can vary significantly. Total expense ratios typically range from as low as 0.03% per year for broad market ETFs to 0.40% per year or more for specialized or niche ETFs. While the difference may seem small, it adds up over time. Lower costs mean that more of your money stays invested, boosting your long-term returns. Always check the expense ratio before investing and weigh it against the ETF's potential returns.

4. Method of Replication

ETFs replicate the performance of their underlying assets through either physical or synthetic replication.

- **Physical Replication.** It involves the ETF holding the actual assets in the index. For example, an ETF that tracks the S&P 500 physically owns all or most of the stocks in that index. This method is straightforward and very safe because the assets are directly owned by the ETF. Physical replication can take two forms: full replication, where the ETF holds every single asset in the index in the exact proportion as the index; and sampling replication, where the ETF holds a representative sample of the index's components. Sampling is often used for larger or more complex indexes, where replicating every asset might be impractical or too costly. The selected sample is carefully designed to closely match the performance of the entire index.

- **Synthetic Replication.** Synthetic replication works differently from physical replication, as the ETF does not directly hold the underlying assets of the index it tracks. Instead, the ETF provider purchases other assets and enters into a swap agreement with a financial institution (the counterparty). In this arrangement, the ETF provider exchanges the returns from the assets it holds for the returns of the index it aims to replicate. This method allows the ETF to synthetically track the performance of the index. Synthetic replication is often used for niche or hard-to-access markets that would be expensive or impractical for the ETF provider to replicate physically. However, it involves counterparty risk: if the financial institution providing the swap defaults, the ETF could incur significant losses or even face default. The counterparty risk makes synthetic ETFs inherently riskier than physically replicated ETFs.

5. Currency Risks

If an ETF holds assets denominated in a foreign currency, its performance will be affected not only by the price movements of those assets, but also by currency fluctuations relative to your base currency. For example, if you invest in a U.S. equity ETF and your base currency is the euro, a weakening of the dollar against the euro may reduce your returns. Some ETFs offer currency-hedged versions that use derivatives to neutralize currency fluctuations. While this can stabilize returns, it also adds costs. Long-term investors often accept currency risk as part of diversification.

6. Accumulation vs. Distribution ETFs

ETFs can handle dividend and interest payments in one of two ways:

- **Accumulation.** These ETFs automatically reinvest dividends and interest back into the fund. This reinvestment adds to the power of compounding and defers taxation until the ETF is sold. Accumulation ETFs are well-suited for long-term investors who prioritize growth over immediate income. By automatically reinvesting dividends and interest, these ETFs maximize the power of compounding while offering greater tax efficiency, making them an excellent choice for building wealth over time.

- **Distribution.** These ETFs regularly pay dividends and interest to investors. These payouts can be useful for those seeking regular income, such as retirees. However, distribution ETFs have two significant drawbacks. First, they are less tax-efficient, as taxes are often due immediately on the payouts. Second, they limit the ability to fully leverage the power of compounding, since the earnings are distributed rather than reinvested automatically.

A Powerful Tool for Exploring ETFs

To explore the wide range of ETFs and understand their characteristics, I highly recommend using the website JustETF.com. This exceptional tool allows you to search for ETFs across all asset classes, review their key features and historical performance, and apply detailed filters. Whether you're a beginner or a seasoned investor, JustETF provides invaluable insights to help you research and select the right ETFs for your portfolio.

Speaking of portfolios, in the next chapters we delve into portfolio construction and management. A savvy lazy investor knows how to combine different types of ETFs to effectively balance risk and maximize returns. Stay tuned, as now we explore how to build and manage a successful investment portfolio.

PART III: The Lazy Investor's Portfolio

Chapter 7: Building a Lazy Investor's Portfolio

Disclaimer

Before delving into the principles of building a balanced portfolio and discussing the types of assets you might include, it's important to clarify some important concepts. The information in this chapter (and throughout all this book) is for educational and informational purposes only. It does not constitute financial advice, nor should it be taken as a personal recommendation on how to allocate your capital. Investing is very personal, and your decisions should reflect your unique circumstances, goals, and risk tolerance. While the concepts and examples presented in this section of the book are intended to provide you with the knowledge and tools to construct a balanced portfolio, the responsibility for managing your money rests with you. The information presented here is grounded in proven principles, but it's ultimately up to you to decide how to apply them, ensuring that your portfolio aligns with your unique financial journey and goals. Always do your own research, consult credible sources, and, if necessary, work with a financial advisor who shares your goals.

Risk-Reward Ratio and Correlation Among Assets

As you already know, one of the foundational principles of investing is the risk-reward ratio. Every asset you include in your portfolio carries a specific level of risk, directly tied to the potential return it can offer. Generally, the higher the risk, the greater the potential reward, and vice versa. Understanding this principle is crucial when building your portfolio. For example, a single stock can be highly risky, especially if it's a small-cap stock from a young, volatile company. In contrast, a stock from a well-established large-cap company generally carries lower risk, albeit with a potentially smaller upside. Diversifying your holdings across 20 different stocks can significantly reduce the risk compared to owning just one, offering a more balanced approach to portfolio management. Continuing with examples, investing in Equity ETFs significantly reduces risk by diversifying across a broad basket of companies. Assets like Bitcoin represent extremely high-risk, high-reward investments. While their value can skyrocket in a short period, they are equally susceptible to steep declines. In contrast, government bonds from stable countries are much safer but typically offer more modest returns. These examples underscore the importance of carefully weighing potential gains against the associated risks when selecting assets for your portfolio.

In addition to assessing individual assets' risk-reward ratios, you need to consider how the assets in your portfolio interact with each other. This is where correlation comes into play. Assets that are highly correlated tend to move in the same direction under similar conditions, which can increase your overall portfolio risk. Conversely, decorrelated assets move independently or even in opposite directions, helping to balance your portfolio and reduce volatility. Take gold, for example. It's often considered a "safe haven" because it tends to perform well during global economic downturns or market crashes. When stock markets are thriving, gold price often declines, but during a crisis, gold can act as a stabilizer. This decorrelation makes gold a valuable addition to a portfolio with a strong presence of stocks or Equity ETFs. As a final example, the relationship between bonds and stocks can vary depending on the type of stocks and bonds, the region, and the prevailing macroeconomic environment. Depending on economic drivers such as central bank policies or inflation trends, bonds and stocks can either move in opposite directions or align with one another.

When constructing your portfolio, always evaluate the risk-reward profiles of the assets you include. Equally important is considering how these assets correlate with one another and how those correlations may evolve over time. By diversifying wisely and incorporating decorrelated assets, you can protect yourself from market fluctuations while maximizing your potential for long-term growth.

Principles of a Balanced Portfolio

Building a balanced portfolio requires adhering to several key principles that safeguard your capital and optimize growth potential. Let's explore the fundamental guidelines you should always keep in mind:

1. <u>Cash Emergency Fund First</u>

Before investing in any asset, ensure you have set aside a sufficient cash emergency fund, as discussed in Chapter 2. This emergency fund acts as a financial safety net, covering your living expenses for a specified period (e.g., 6 months) in case of unexpected events. Only once this reserve is fully established should you allocate funds toward building your investment portfolio.

2. <u>The Liquidity Rule</u>

Beyond your cash emergency fund, maintaining additional liquidity within your portfolio is crucial. This principle, which I call the "liquidity rule", ensures that your portfolio includes a cushion of cash or low-risk assets to counterbalance higher-risk investments, such as cryptocurrencies. Unlike your emergency fund, this cash cushion is an integral part of your portfolio. It should range between 1x and 2x the value of your riskiest assets, depending on your risk tolerance. For example, if 10% of your portfolio is allocated to very high-risk assets like cryptocurrencies, you should hold at least 10% to 20% of your portfolio in cash or ultra-safe assets, such as government bonds from stable countries.

3. Asset Allocation

One of the most important steps in constructing a balanced portfolio is determining how to allocate your investments across various asset classes. While there's no one-size-fits-all answer, below are my general guidelines and principles to help you create a diversified and well-balanced portfolio. These are general suggestions, not financial advice, so always make decisions based on your personal goals, risk tolerance, and financial situation.

Stocks and Equity ETFs

Stocks and Equity ETFs are the primary growth drivers in any portfolio. These assets should typically constitute between 50% and 80% of your portfolio, depending on your risk tolerance and financial goals. If you choose to pursue value investing as detailed earlier in this book, Warren Buffett suggests focusing on only 5 to 10 carefully selected companies[13]. I fully agree with this approach, as it allows you to deeply understand each company, monitor them closely, and make more informed decisions. Within this allocation, it's crucial to diversify across geographic areas to minimize risk. For example, a well-diversified portfolio might include:

- 50% in U.S. companies.
- 30% in European companies.
- 20% in Asian companies, including emerging markets.

Also, ensure that the companies you select operate in different sectors, preferably ones that are as decorrelated as possible.

As you already know, Equity ETFs are a better option for lazy investors. A potential allocation might look like this:

- 50% in a S&P 500 ETF for U.S. exposure.

---

[13] **Buffett, W. (2019).** *The Essays of Warren Buffett: Lessons for Corporate America.* Edited by Lawrence A. Cunningham, 5th ed., Wiley, 2019.

- 30% in a Europe 600 ETF, which covers the largest 600 companies in Europe.
- 20% in an Asia Emerging Markets ETF.

Alternatively, you might explore ETFs like World ETFs, which offer global diversification in a single product. You could also look into region-specific ETFs targeting mature Asian markets, such as Australia, Hong Kong, or Singapore. For those interested in emerging markets, specialized ETFs focusing exclusively on specific countries, such as China, are also worth considering.

You can also combine both approaches by holding a mix of individual stocks and Equity ETFs. However, remember that individual stocks always carry higher risks compared to Equity ETFs. In any case, one of my personal guiding principles is to allocate 50% of the equity portion to U.S. markets, with the remaining 50% distributed across other markets. You can adjust the non-U.S. portion based on your risk tolerance, either favoring emerging markets for higher risk and potential returns or opting for more mature markets like Europe for greater stability.

Cryptocurrencies

While highly volatile, cryptocurrencies have the potential to deliver significant returns. For this asset class, your portfolio allocation might range between 5% and 30%, depending on your risk tolerance. If you're new to crypto investing, a simple and effective allocation strategy is to dedicate at least 70% of your allocation to Bitcoin (BTC), and up to 30% to Ethereum (ETH). For a more comprehensive understanding of why and how to include cryptocurrencies in your portfolio, I recommend exploring my book *"Cryptocurrency Investing"*.

Cash, Bonds and Bond ETFs

As discussed earlier, it's essential to consistently apply what I call "the liquidity rule" when constructing your portfolio. This rule emphasizes maintaining a safety net of secure assets—such as government bond from stable countries, government bonds ETFs from stable countries, or cash—to counterbalance high-risk investments. Specifically, for every dollar allocated to high-risk assets, consider allocating an additional 1x to 2x of that value to these safer categories. How much should you allocate to cash or highly secure assets overall? A general guideline is to dedicate 5% to 40% of your portfolio to these safer assets, depending on the risk level of your other holdings. Personally, I always recommend linking this allocation directly to cryptocurrencies. For example, if you allocate 10% of your portfolio to crypto, consider holding an additional 10% to 20% in cash or government bonds (or government bond ETFs) from stable countries as a counterbalance. This approach ensures a layer of stability while allowing you to explore higher-risk opportunities.

Regardless of the "liquidity rule," any bonds you include in your portfolio should be carefully evaluated based on macroeconomic conditions, inflation trends, and central bank policies. Some bonds can at times correlate closely with equity markets, reducing their value as a diversification tool. When considering bonds, it's essential to account for these dynamics to ensure they align with your overall portfolio strategy and risk tolerance. If this level of analysis feels overwhelming, prioritizing cash remains a straightforward and effective way to balance riskier investments like cryptocurrencies.

Commodities and Precious Metals

What's missing? Commodities, including precious metals. These assets are valuable for diversifying your portfolio, with a typical allocation ranging from 5% to 30%. Gold, often regarded as a "safe haven," should make up the majority of this allocation due to its ability to counterbalance stocks during periods of economic downturns and market volatility. A smaller portion can be allocated to other commodities, such as silver or oil, depending on your investment objectives and market expectations.

4. The Importance of Macroeconomic Conditions

Another key principle is considering adjustments to your portfolio to align with market cycles and broader macroeconomic trends. During periods of economic optimism or bull markets, you might consider slightly increasing your allocation to stocks and other riskier assets to take advantage of growth opportunities. Conversely, in bear markets or times of economic uncertainty, you could strengthen your cash cushion or allocate more to safer investments like bonds or gold. These adjustments should be made cautiously and incrementally to avoid straying too far from the long-term focus of your investment strategy. The objective isn't to time the market but to fine-tune your portfolio in response to evolving conditions, ensuring it remains well balanced over time.

Full Example of a Medium-High Risk Portfolio for a Lazy Investor

Before diving into the example, let me reiterate that this is for educational purposes only and should not be taken as investment advice. Every portfolio should be tailored to individual circumstances, goals, and risk tolerance. With that in mind, the following is a general example of a balanced portfolio designed for a lazy investor with medium-to-high risk tolerance:

1. **Cryptocurrency: 15%.** This portfolio allocates 15% to cryptocurrencies, with 12% of that allocation dedicated to Bitcoin (BTC) and 3% to Ethereum (ETH).

2. **Cash: 15%.** This matches the cryptocurrency allocation, adhering to the "liquidity rule".

3. **Equity ETFs: 60%.** They represent the growth engine of the portfolio. Remember to always choose accumulating ETFs, where dividends and interests are automatically reinvested, to maximize compounding over the long term. In this portfolio, the 60% equity allocation is diversified across three distinct Equity ETFs:

   - 30% in a S&P 500 ETF.
   - 15% in a Europe 600 ETF.
   - 15% in an Asia Emerging Market ETF.

4. **Gold ETF: 10%.** The remaining 10% is allocated to a gold ETF, a reliable safe-haven asset that helps balance risk during periods of economic instability.

This portfolio does not include bonds, primarily due to the reasons discussed earlier: their correlation with stocks varies significantly based on the macroeconomic conditions, inflation trends, and central banks policies. This variability makes it challenging to incorporate them into a generalized example. Nonetheless, if you wish to add bonds, you could consider reducing the cash allocation to invest in low-risk assets like government bonds from stable countries. Higher-risk bonds with greater risk-reward potential could also be included. However, in this case as well, you must have a solid understanding of their correlation with equities and the current phase of the economic cycle.

Chapter 8: DCA and Portfolio Management

Dollar-Cost Averaging (DCA)

Congratulations! You've learned how to create a balanced long-term investment portfolio tailored to your lazy investor mindset. But how do you actually begin investing? One of the most effective and widely used methods is Dollar-Cost Averaging (DCA). This approach involves systematically investing a fixed amount of money in your chosen assets at regular intervals, regardless of market conditions. By spreading out your investments, DCA helps to smooth the impact of market fluctuations, allowing you to avoid the risks of investing a lump sum at the wrong time. Let's take an example. Suppose you have $10,000 to invest. Instead of committing it all at once, you decide to invest $2,000 each month over the next five months. On the first of each month, you purchase an equal portion of your chosen assets. This approach safeguards you from the risk of investing the entire amount at a market peak.

DCA is not only a strategy for deploying a lump sum but also a great way to invest your savings over time. For instance, you could decide to allocate 20% of your monthly income, or a fixed amount that aligns with your budget, towards building your portfolio. This approach ensures consistent growth while fostering better financial discipline. Instead of spending first and investing what's left, you reverse the process: prioritize your monthly investments and spend only what remains. It's a subtle but powerful mindset shift that can transform your financial habits.

When implementing DCA, you should consider a few key aspects. First, determine how often you'll invest. Monthly contributions are a common choice because they align with most income cycles. It's also essential to evaluate the composition of your portfolio. A portfolio with too many assets can lead to higher transaction costs since you'll need to buy each asset separately at regular intervals. This is where ETFs are especially advantageous. With just a few ETFs, you can achieve broad diversification without incurring excessive costs or complications in portfolio management.

Another advantage of DCA is its flexibility. If unexpected expenses arise and your cash reserves need replenishing, you can temporarily reduce your contributions. Conversely, if you find yourself with extra funds in a specific month, you can choose to allocate more to your investments. This adaptability ensures that your financial situation is always considered while keeping your long-term investment goals on track. DCA is an excellent strategy for gradually building your portfolio, and it also pairs seamlessly with portfolio rebalancing to maintain optimal asset allocation. Over time, market movements can shift the balance of your investments, and periodic adjustments are necessary to ensure your portfolio remains aligned with your goals and risk tolerance. In the next chapter, we'll delve deeper into strategies for optimizing your portfolio over time.

Portfolio Rebalancing

Portfolio rebalancing is a fundamental investment management practice that ensures your portfolio remains aligned with your original strategy and risk tolerance over time. As market dynamics fluctuate, the value of individual assets within your portfolio will inevitably change, causing deviations from your original allocations. Rebalancing allows you to restore your portfolio to its intended balance, optimizing returns while effectively managing risk.

Let's revisit the example of a medium-high risk portfolio for a lazy investor: 15% in cryptocurrencies, 15% in cash, 60% in Equity ETFs (30% S&P 500, 15% Europe 600, 15% Asia Emerging Markets), and 10% in a gold ETF. Imagine that after several months of market activity, Bitcoin (BTC) surges, growing to 25% of your portfolio. This imbalance now exposes your portfolio to higher volatility due to the increased weight of BTC. To rebalance, you could sell a portion of your BTC holdings and redirect the proceeds into cash or underweighted assets like equity ETFs. This adjustment helps restore your portfolio to its original proportions, ensuring it remains aligned with your investment strategy and risk tolerance. Alternatively (and this is the preferred approach) you could use your next monthly DCA contributions toward the underweighted assets instead of selling the overperforming assets. This strategy can achieve the same goal of restoring balance while avoiding taxable events triggered by asset sales. However, this works best if your monthly contributions are not too small compared to your overall portfolio. If they are, you can still achieve balance by consistently allocating them to the underweighted assets over several months, gradually bringing your portfolio back into alignment.

To rebalance your portfolio effectively and efficiently, follow these guidelines:

1. **Establish a Rebalancing Schedule.** Popular rebalancing intervals include quarterly, semi-annual, or annual reviews. Avoid rebalancing too frequently, as this can lead to excessive transaction costs and tax liabilities.

2. **Set a Tolerance Level.** Perfection isn't necessary when it comes to rebalancing. Allow your portfolio to deviate slightly from your target allocations before taking action. For example, you might decide to rebalance only if an asset deviates 5% or more from its intended allocation. This reduces unnecessary trading and minimizes costs.

3. **Use DCA for Rebalancing.** As discussed earlier, when you make regular DCA contributions to your portfolio, you can use those contributions strategically to rebalance. For example, instead of selling overperforming assets, you can use your DCA funds to buy underperforming or underweighted assets. This approach minimizes sales, which reduces both fees and tax consequences.

4. **Differentiate Between Asset Classes and Subcategories.** You can adopt different rebalancing strategies for asset classes and their subcategories. For example, within cryptocurrencies (an asset class), Bitcoin (BTC) and Ethereum (ETH) can be treated as subcategories, allowing you to rebalance their allocations more frequently, such as quarterly. In contrast, the overall portfolio allocation across asset classes—like Equity ETFs, cryptocurrencies, and Commodity ETFs—might only require rebalancing once or twice a year. Additionally, be mindful of transaction fees and tax implications, which can vary depending on the assets being adjusted.

5. **Keep Accurate Records.** Keep detailed records of all rebalancing activities, either in a spreadsheet or by using investment tracking tools. This documentation will help you monitor your portfolio's performance and evaluate whether your strategy requires adjustments. Portfolio management apps can streamline this process, offering valuable insights into asset performance and ensuring your investments stay aligned with your goals.

Tax Efficiency Made Easy

Tax efficiency is a critical aspect of managing an investment portfolio, as taxes can have a significant impact on your overall returns. One of the most effective ways to reduce your tax liability is to limit the frequency of asset sales at a profit in your portfolio. Each time you sell an asset at a profit, capital gains taxes are triggered, reducing your overall returns. By using strategies such as DCA for rebalancing, you can keep taxable events to a minimum. Moreover, ETFs are particularly advantageous for tax-efficient investing. Choosing accumulation ETFs, which reinvest dividends and interest back into the fund rather than distributing them to investors, will let you avoid immediate tax obligations. This allows your investment to grow uninterrupted, increasing the long-term compounding effect. In addition, keeping your portfolio simple and streamlined is another effective way to optimize for tax efficiency. A portfolio with fewer, carefully selected assets is easier to manage and rebalance without triggering frequent taxable events. This simplicity not only saves taxes, but also fits the lazy investor philosophy of minimal effort.

Long-term investing is often closely linked to tax efficiency. In many countries, holding assets for an extended period qualifies investors for favorable tax treatment, such as reduced capital gains tax rates for investments retained beyond a specified number of years. However, tax laws are complex and vary significantly by jurisdiction. To optimize your investment strategy for tax efficiency, it's advisable to consult a qualified financial or tax advisor familiar with your country's regulations.

PART IV: The Lazy Trader's Strategies

Chapter 9: Understanding Day Trading

Can you help us? If you like the book, please leave a review on Amazon by scanning the following QR code with your smartphone. For you it is a matter of seconds, but for us it is invaluable. Thank you in advance!

Also, if you're interested in taking your wealth to the next level, check out *Crypto Go Wealth Accelerator.* It's available only a few times a year. Scan the QR code below to learn more:

What is Day Trading?

As discussed in Chapter 3, day trading involves buying and selling financial assets within the same trading day in order to profit from small price fluctuations. Unlike investing, which typically focuses on long-term capital appreciation, day trading is all about quick transactions and short time frames. Positions are never held overnight; each trade is opened and closed during the same trading session. Day traders seek to exploit volatility by using tools and techniques to predict how prices will move in the very short term. Successful day traders often rely on technical analysis, which involves studying price charts, patterns, trends, and indicators to make trading decisions. Because the time frame is so short, even minor price fluctuations can be the difference between profit and loss, particularly when trading derivatives like Contract for Differences (CFDs), which we will discuss shortly.

One of the key aspects of day trading is the use of leverage, enabling traders to open larger positions with only a small amount of capital. In contrast, value investing typically does not involve leverage. While leveraging can boost potential profits, it also heightens risk. For this reason, day traders must be vigilant about managing their exposure and implementing stringent risk management measures. Common practices include setting stop-loss orders to cap potential losses on individual trades, as well as placing take-profit orders to lock in gains.

Best Assets for Day Trading

The best assets for day trading are those that have high liquidity, substantial capitalization, and sufficient volatility to allow for frequent price movements in short time frames. Below are the most commonly used asset classes for day trading:

Forex (Foreign Exchange Market)

The Forex market is one of the world's most popular and liquid trading venues, making it particularly well-suited for day trading. With operations running 24 hours a day, five days a week, it offers traders around the globe exceptional flexibility. The market's inherent volatility and responsiveness to macroeconomic news create frequent opportunities for short-term trading strategies.

Cryptocurrencies

Cryptocurrencies appeal to day traders because they're available 24/7 and often exhibit significant volatility. Among them, well-capitalized assets like Bitcoin (BTC) and Ethereum (ETH) stand out. Their larger market cap and higher trading volumes tend to produce more consistent price patterns, making technical analysis more meaningful. In contrast, smaller, thinly traded altcoins are highly speculative and prone to erratic price swings, where traditional technical analysis often provides limited guidance. However, these smaller altcoins can present extraordinary short-term trading opportunities that rely not on technical analysis, but rather on a specialized approach called "On-Chain Analysis". This advanced method uses blockchain data to identify the best moments for successful short-term trades. It's a unique trading methodology that I explore in detail in my book "*Cryptocurrency Investing*".

Stocks

Day traders often focus on stocks that are both highly liquid and capable of significant short-term price movements. Larger, well-established companies typically offer smoother trade execution and high daily trading volumes, though their price swings may be more moderate. In contrast, smaller or lesser-known stocks can be significantly more volatile, potentially offering quick profits. However, they are often less liquid and inherently riskier.

Commodities

Gold, silver, crude oil, and other commodities are also popular for day trading due to their price sensitivity to macroeconomic events and shifts in supply and demand.

ETFs

Although many ETFs may exhibit relatively moderate volatility compared to individual stocks, certain sector or theme-specific ETFs can still experience sharper intraday price movements.

Derivatives: Futures and Contracts for Difference (CFDs)

Very often, day traders do not engage directly with the assets described above. Instead, they turn to derivatives, particularly Futures and CFDs. As you already know, these instruments allow traders to leverage their capital, making it possible to control larger positions with a relatively small initial investment.

Futures are standardized contracts that obligate the buyer and seller to exchange an underlying asset, such as commodities or currencies, at a predetermined price and date in the future. With CFDs, the trader enters into an agreement with a broker to exchange the difference in the value of an asset between the time the contract is opened and when it is closed. If the price moves in the trader's favor, they earn a profit based on the price difference. Conversely, if the price moves against them, they incur a loss. CFDs offer flexibility, as they can be used to speculate on both rising (long positions) and falling (short positions) markets, making them a versatile tool for day trading. However, they also involve significant risks, especially when leverage is applied, amplifying both potential profits and losses. Due to the costs associated with CFDs, such as spreads and overnight financing fees, which can accumulate quickly, and the potential for leverage to magnify small price fluctuations into significant swings in account equity, disciplined risk management is crucial for anyone trading CFDs. Additionally, since regulations governing CFD trading vary by jurisdiction, it is essential for traders to familiarize themselves with local rules before executing trades on CFDs.

Technical Analysis Basics

Every day trader should have a basic understanding of technical analysis. While this book does not aim to delve into the intricate details of technical analysis, it is essential to understand the basic concepts. Here are the five essential concepts in technical analysis: Japanese candlesticks, support, resistance, trendlines, and moving averages. Each plays a crucial role in understanding price action and helps you identify potential entry and exit points as a day trader.

1. Japanese Candlesticks

Japanese candlesticks are a charting method developed centuries ago by Japanese rice traders, and they remain one of the most widely used tools in modern technical analysis. Each candlestick represents a set time period and provides visual insight into the market's open, close, high, and low prices. By observing the shape, color, and relative position of these candles, traders can quickly gauge market sentiment (whether buyers or sellers are dominant) and spot patterns that may signal reversals or continuations in price trends.

2. Supports

Support is a price level at which an asset's downward movement tends to stop or reverse because demand begins to outweigh supply. Think of support as a floor that "supports" the price. Traders often look for support levels to identify potential buying opportunities. A break below a support could signal further downward movement, so it's also a critical area for placing stop-loss orders.

Figure 1: Example of a Support Level on a Japanese Candlestick Chart

Source: BTC/USD, TradingView

3. Resistances

Resistance is the opposite of support. It marks a price level where an asset's upward movement frequently stalls or reverses due to an increase in selling pressure. In other words, resistance acts like a ceiling that the price struggles to penetrate. Traders commonly use resistance levels to identify profit-taking targets or to initiate short positions. When the price does break above a resistance level, it often signals a significant surge in bullish strength and can mark the start of a new upward trend.

Figure 2: Example of a Resistance Level on a Japanese Candlestick Chart

Source: BTC/USD, TradingView

4. Trendlines

Trendlines are diagonal lines drawn on a price chart to illustrate the general direction of an asset's price movement over time. They come in two main varieties: uptrend lines and downtrend lines. An uptrend line is drawn by connecting a series of "higher lows". These are points where the price dips during an upward movement but doesn't fall as low as the previous pullback, suggesting that buyers are steadily driving the price higher. Conversely, a downtrend line is formed by linking a series of "lower highs". These are points where the price rises during a downward movement but never reaches the previous peak, indicating that sellers are maintaining control and pushing the price lower. Trendlines are essential tools for visualizing trends, spotting potential reversal areas, and finding possible entry and exit points based on how the price interacts with the drawn line.

5. <u>Moving Averages</u>

A Moving Average (MA) smooths price data to help identify trends. It calculates the average price of an asset over a specified period of time, such as 10, 21, 50 or 200 days (or another period of time). The two most common types of moving averages are:

- **Simple Moving Average (SMA):** An average of the price over a period of time.

- **Exponential Moving Average (EMA):** Gives more weight to recent prices, making it more sensitive to recent price changes.

Moving averages can act as dynamic support or resistance levels. They also provide signals when shorter-term moving averages cross longer-term moving averages. For example, a "golden cross" occurs when a short-term moving average crosses above a long-term moving average, signaling a potential uptrend and a possible long signal. Conversely, when a short-term moving average crosses below a long-term moving average, often referred to as a "death cross," it signals a potential downtrend and can serve as a possible short signal.

Figure 4: Example of a "Golden Cross" as a 10-Day SMA Crosses Above a 50-Day SMA on a Japanese Candlestick Chart

Source: BTC/USD, TradingView

Five Popular Day Trading Strategies

Below are five commonly used and highly popular day trading strategies. Each approach can be adapted to various assets and market conditions, but it's crucial to consider the most appropriate time frame for your particular market. For example, many day traders find success using 5- or 15-minute charts, as these shorter intervals often reveal clearer intraday trends and opportunities. Experimenting with different timeframes is strongly recommended, as finding the one best suited not only to the asset you're trading but also to your own trading style and mindset can significantly improve your results.

1. <u>Support and Resistance Trading</u>

Building on the concepts introduced earlier, this strategy centers on identifying established support and resistance levels. The goal is to enter a long position near support, where buyers have historically stepped in, and to close that position near resistance, where selling pressure has tended to emerge. Conversely, short trades can be initiated near resistance levels and closed around support. By using these familiar benchmarks, traders aim to capitalize on predictable patterns in price behavior.

How to Apply This Strategy:

- Open your chart and find clear support and resistance levels based on past price behavior.

- Wait for the price to approach one of these levels. If the price approaches a support, open a long position. If it approaches a resistance, go short.

- Set a stop loss just below the support (for long trades) or just above the resistance (for short trades).

- Close your trade as the price approaches the next significant level, such as another resistance level for long positions or another support level for short positions.

2. Moving Average Crossover

This strategy uses two moving averages, typically one short-term (e.g. 10 periods) and one longer-term (e.g. 50 periods), to identify trend changes. A buy signal or an exit from a short trade is triggered when the short-term moving average crosses above the long-term moving average ("Golden Cross"). Conversely, when the short-term average crosses below the long-term average, it signals an opportunity to open a short trade or exit an existing long position ("Death Cross").

How to Apply This Strategy:

- Add two exponential moving averages (EMAs) to your chart: a fast one (e.g. 9 periods) and a slow one (e.g. 21 periods). Experiment with different EMA settings to find the combination that best suits the specific asset you are trading.

- Open a long position when the fast EMA crosses above the slow EMA. Go short when the fast EMA crosses below the slow EMA.

- Exit the trade at the next opposite crossover.

3. Breakout Trading

Breakout trading involves taking advantage of price movements when the price "breaks out" of a predetermined range or level. The breakout is often accompanied by high volume, indicating strong market interest.

How to Apply This Strategy:

- Identify an important support or resistance level from which the price has repeatedly bounced.

- Wait for the price to break through this level with high volume.

- Enter a long trade when the price breaks resistance or a short trade when it breaks support.

- Place a stop loss just below (long) or just above (short) the breakout level.

- Take profits near the next identified support or resistance level.

4. RSI Divergence Trading

RSI Divergence Trading is based on the Relative Strength Index (RSI), a widely used momentum oscillator that measures the speed and magnitude of recent price movements. The RSI typically ranges from 0 to 100, with readings above 70 often considered overbought and below 30 considered oversold. When the RSI and price action move in opposite directions—known as a divergence—it frequently indicates that the current trend is losing steam and may soon reverse. Recognizing these divergences can help traders enter or exit positions before a major turning point occurs.

How to Apply This Strategy:

- Apply the RSI to your chosen time frame, marking its overbought and oversold levels.

- Look for a bullish divergence, where price makes new lows but the RSI does not, suggesting a possible upward reversal.

- Identify bearish divergences when price reaches new highs but the RSI fails to do so, indicating a potential downward reversal.

- Enter a long position once a bullish divergence is confirmed, or enter a short position when a bearish divergence is confirmed.

- Set both your stop loss and take profit orders near previously identified support or resistance levels.

Figure 5: Example of a Bearish Divergence on a Japanese Candlestick Chart

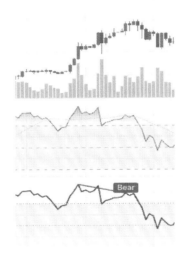

Source: BTC/USD, TradingView

5. Scalping with Trendlines

Scalping involves taking advantage of very small price movements throughout the day. Using trendlines helps to identify short-term directional bias and quick entry/exit points.

How to Apply This Strategy:

- Draw trendlines connecting the highs in a downtrend and the lows in an uptrend.

- Trade along the trend by entering near the trendline. In an up-trend, consider opening long positions near the trendline and exiting as the price reaches a new high. In a downtrend, consider opening short positions near the trendline and exiting as the price makes a new low.

- Use tight stop-losses and place them just outside the trendline.

Executing Day Trades

The strategies outlined above can be executed in two primary ways: manually or using preset orders. With manual execution, you open and close trades yourself, relying on real-time analysis of price movements and technical signals. This hands-on approach keeps you deeply engaged with the market and allows for quick adjustments to changing conditions. However, it requires constant focus, discipline, and the ability to manage emotions effectively. That said, even when trading manually, it's highly advisable to always set stop-loss orders. These act as a safety net, limiting potential losses in case the market moves against your position.

For traders seeking a more structured and less emotionally driven approach, preset orders offer a practical alternative. At the beginning of the trading session, you determine your entry levels, stop-loss points, and take-profit targets, based on your preferred strategy. By doing this, you set the stage for trades to be triggered automatically at predetermined price levels. However, if you simply set these orders and walk away, you are unlikely to achieve consistent results. Strategies evolve alongside market conditions, and it's crucial to monitor their performance. If necessary, you should adjust your preset orders to align with any changes in the market or your strategy's requirements. Active oversight, even with preset orders, remains a key component of successful day trading.

Whichever method you employ, effective risk management and strict adherence to your established rules remain paramount. Even the most carefully crafted strategy can fail if position sizes are not controlled, stop-loss orders are ignored, or profit targets are set unrealistically.

Chapter 10: Why Day Trading (Almost Always) Sucks for Lazy Traders

After covering day trading and technical analysis, it's time to confront a simple truth: day trading is often a terrible fit for most people. This chapter explains why the dream of becoming a successful day trader is, in nearly all cases, a misguided aspiration, even though the previous sections provided you with the foundational knowledge to attempt it. I strongly advise against pursuing this path. In the following pages, we'll dissect the reasons why so few individuals are truly suited for day trading.

Why 90% of Day Traders Lose Money

The harsh reality of day trading is that 90% of those who try it lose money. Before you jump in, ask yourself if it's really worth it to engage in an activity where the odds of success are so stacked against you. Why is day trading so unforgiving, even for those who are diligent and willing to put in the work? Let's explore the main reasons. A major factor is information asymmetry. In almost every financial market, retail day traders like you are at a significant disadvantage compared to institutional players. These large firms have access to information unavailable to the average trader, including advanced market data, proprietary research, and insider connections. They use their superior knowledge to make decisions that retail traders cannot anticipate, often moving markets in ways that work against smaller players.

Trading algorithms and bots pose another significant challenge. Large firms and institutional traders use sophisticated automated systems capable of executing trades at lightning speed, analyzing vast amounts of data, and predicting price movements with unparalleled accuracy. These bots often exploit small inefficiencies in the market, effectively outmaneuvering human day traders. Even worse, some of these systems are designed to manipulate the behavior of retail traders, driving prices into traps that inexperienced traders fall into, resulting in heavy losses.

Finally, there's the issue of human emotion. Day trading is an incredibly stressful and fast-paced activity, and emotions such as fear and greed can cloud your judgment and lead to poor decisions. When faced with losses, fear can cause you to exit trades prematurely, locking in losses instead of giving your strategy time to work. On the other hand, greed can lead you to hold onto winning trades for too long, only to see your profits evaporate when the market reverses. Even seasoned professionals struggle to manage these psychological pressures, and they often have teams and tools to help mitigate the risks. The combination of these factors creates an almost insurmountable barrier for most retail day traders.

The Typical Day of a Day Trader

Have you ever wondered what life as a day trader is really like? Maybe you picture glamorous scenes of quick trades, massive profits, and carefree afternoons sipping cocktails by the pool. Reality check: it's nothing like that. Instead, the life of a day trader is an emotional roller coaster filled with stress, self-doubt, and endless screen time. To give you a better idea, here's a step-by-step look at a typical day in the life of a US stocks day trader—one where things don't go quite as planned. You'll quickly realize that it's far from the dream job many imagine!

6:00 AM – The pre-market hustle

Your alarm clock jolts you awake and you stumble out of bed. The markets haven't even opened yet, but you're already glued to your phone, scanning the pre-market conditions. Forums, news feeds and self-appointed trading gurus flood your brain with ticker symbols and "hot tips". You sip coffee and convince yourself: today is the day I make it big.

9:30 AM - Market opens, chaos ensues

The bell rings and your screen explodes with activity. Charts dance, lines zigzag, and your heart races. You execute your first trade, confident that your strategy is sound. Two minutes later, the stock takes a nosedive. You panic and sell at a loss, only to see it rebound moments later. Frustrated, you jump to another trade, only to face the same disheartening outcome.

12:00 noon - The lunch that never comes

You're getting hungry, but you don't dare leave your desk. What if you miss a great opportunity? You stare at candlestick charts, trying to decipher patterns while your stomach growls in protest. By now you've made a few trades, most of them losing money. You tell yourself it's just bad luck.

2:00 PM - Desperation sets in

The clock is ticking and your losses are mounting. You double down on a risky trade to make up for the morning's disasters. For a brief moment, it works, and your account balance rises. Then, just as quickly, the stock reverses. Your gains evaporate, and you're left staring at the screen in disbelief.

4:00 PM - Market closes, regret begins

The closing bell rings. You're exhausted, both emotionally and financially. Your account balance is lower than when you started, and you're wondering why you are doing this job. But hey, tomorrow's another day, right? You'll do better. At least that's what you tell yourself.

Hidden Costs

If everything we've discussed so far isn't enough to dissuade you from diving into day trading, let me make one final argument: the hidden costs. These are the often-overlooked expenses, financial and personal, that can turn your day trading dream into a draining nightmare. First, the financial costs. For example, trading CFDs may seem appealing because of the leverage, but you'll soon realize how much you're paying in spreads and fees. Even in traditional markets, commissions can add up quickly if you're making multiple trades each day. A small fee per trade may sound trivial, but if you're making dozens of trades a day, it can quietly erode your account balance. Then there's slippage, the difference between the price you expect and the price your order actually fills, a cost that retail traders often underestimate in derivatives like CFDs.

But even these financial drains pale in comparison to the ultimate hidden cost: your time. Many people are attracted to day trading because it seems to offer freedom. No boss, no set hours, just you and the markets. The reality? It's anything but freeing. Day trading requires constant attention to screens, with every tick of the chart demanding your focus. Even when you're not actively trading, the market is on your mind. You're always thinking about the next setup, the trade you missed, or the strategy you're tweaking. It's like carrying a weight that never lifts, even after the market closes. And it doesn't stop there. Day trading seeps into your personal life. The ups and downs of the market begin to dictate your mood. One bad day can ruin your evening. A string of losses can make you irritable with your loved ones. It's not just your money that's at risk. It's your happiness, your relationships, and your peace of mind.

Ask yourself: is this really the life you want? Day trading may promise excitement and fast profits, but the reality is often a draining cycle of stress, losses and wasted potential. There are smarter, more profitable ways to grow your wealth that don't require sacrificing your time, energy, or well-being. In the next chapter, we'll explore alternative methods of short-term speculation that are far more sustainable, and far more rewarding, than day trading could ever hope to be.

Chapter 11: Lazy (and Smarter) Alternatives to Day Trading

Short-term speculation, especially day trading, comes with its own set of challenges and drawbacks, as we've seen in the previous chapter. But that doesn't mean you should abandon short-term speculative strategies altogether. In fact, there are smarter alternatives to day trading that allow you to profit from market movements without sacrificing your sanity or your entire day. These methods are especially well-suited for those who value efficiency and want their money to work for them with minimal manual effort. In this chapter, we'll explore three excellent substitutes for traditional day trading: Trading Signals, Copy Trading, and Trading BOTs.

Before we dive any deeper, let's address an important question: how much money should you commit to these short-term, high-risk activities? Earlier, we discussed building a long-term portfolio using practices like DCA. This situation calls for a different perspective. Instead of treating these speculative endeavors as part of the long-term investment plan for your savings, consider them entrepreneurial ventures. You set aside a predetermined amount of capital specifically for these high-risk, high-reward trades, fully aware that the outcome may be profitable, or it may not. Unlike your core investment portfolio, where you aim for steady growth over time, this segment operates under a more experimental, business-like approach. You're effectively running a "side enterprise" with its own budget and risk profile, distinct from your stable, long-term investments. Naturally, you can adjust the amount of capital you allocate as you gain experience and refine your strategies. But the key idea remains: separate your short-term speculative funds from your long-term investment assets, and view this portion of your capital as an entrepreneurial stake rather than a standard investment.

Trading Signals

Trading signals are one of the simplest and most convenient alternatives to traditional day trading. Essentially, they're recommendations provided by experienced and professionals traders, those in the top 10% who consistently make money from day trading. These signals typically include suggested entry and exit points for specific assets. They are designed to guide you through the complexities of short-term trading without requiring you to analyze charts or develop your own strategies.

The most common way to access trading signals is through subscription-based services, often hosted on platforms such as Telegram. These groups allow subscribers to receive real-time signals directly from these experienced traders. The beauty of this system is its flexibility. If you find that a particular signal provider isn't delivering satisfactory results, you can simply cancel your subscription and switch to another provider. However, it's generally recommended to test a signal provider's strategy for at least a few months before making a final judgment.

Trading signals are used in a variety of asset classes. While they've become particularly popular in the crypto world due to the market's high volatility and profit potential, they're also widely used in traditional financial markets such as forex, stocks and commodities. Regardless of the asset class, the principle remains the same: you're leveraging the expertise of others to save yourself the time and effort of analyzing the market. Of course, not all signal services are created equal, so it's crucial to choose providers with a strong reputation. While trading signals can't guarantee profits, they are an excellent lazy alternative for those who want to dip their toes into short-term trading without committing to the grind of becoming a full-time day trader.

Copy Trading

Copy trading is another powerful and lazy alternative to traditional day trading. It allows you to automatically replicate the trades of a successful trader, often known as a "Master Trader". Instead of spending countless hours analyzing charts and making trading decisions, you simply allocate your funds to copy the exact positions and trades of the expert. Copy trading is typically facilitated by financial intermediaries or brokers who provide specialized platforms. These platforms allow you to select a trader whose strategy match your investment goals and risk tolerance. Once you've chosen a master trader, the platform does the rest: every trade he makes is reflected in your account in proportion to the amount you've invested. While there's no minimum investment required to copy master traders, many of them recommend maintaining a certain minimum level of liquidity to replicate their trades effectively and avoid the risk of liquidation. Don't worry, though—these thresholds are typically quite low, often ranging between $1,000 and $2,000.

Participating in copy trading typically involves two main costs. The first is a one-time fee required to become a follower of a master trader, granting you access to replicate their trades. The second is a profit-sharing arrangement, where a portion of the profits you generate through copy trading—typically ranging from 10% to 30%—is paid to the master trader. The exact percentage varies based on the platform and the specific master trader you choose to follow. This profit-sharing structure ensures that the master trader is incentivized to perform well as his earnings are directly dependent on your success.

One of the main benefits of copy trading is its unprecedented level of automation. Once you've allocated funds to copy a master trader, there's little else you need to do. The system handles everything from executing trades to distributing profits. It's ideal for those who want exposure to active trading strategies without having to actively participate. Another advantage of copy trading is its flexibility. If for any reason you're not satisfied with the results or strategy of a particular master trader, you can stop copying at any time and withdraw your funds. It's worth noting, however, that just as with trading signals, you should give the strategy enough time to prove itself, ideally a few months, before deciding to stop or move on to another master trader.

While copy trading is common across various asset classes, it is particularly popular in the crypto market due to its high volatility and profit potential. Clearly, it's important to choose a master trader wisely. Look for those with a great reputation and strategies that align with your financial goals. Some master traders execute their trades manually, using their expertise to navigate the market in real time. Others focus on programming and fine-tuning automated trading bots to execute strategies on their behalf. In many cases, these master traders use a blend of both approaches, combining their bots with some manual trades.

Beyond short-term speculation, copy trading is also an exceptional tool for long-term investing. Some platforms allow investors to copy the ETF portfolio of a successful long-term investor, providing a fully automated way to build wealth over time. In this case, you don't even need to research ETFs yourself or manually rebalance your portfolio—the platform mirrors every adjustment made by the "Master Investor". This means that whenever the master investor adds, removes, or rebalances assets, your portfolio automatically follows suit. As a result, copy trading is not just for short-term trading; it is also a powerful wealth-building strategy for long-term investors.

Trading BOTs

Trading bots represent another outstanding lazy alternative to traditional day trading. These automated tools are software programs designed to execute trades based on predefined rules, often related to technical analysis. Once set up, they work around the clock, scanning the market, identifying opportunities and executing trades on your behalf, all without requiring your constant attention. While anyone can technically create a trading bot, it's not as easy as it seems. Successful bots are not just about programming; they require a deep understanding of the markets and technical indicators, as well as the ability to adapt strategies to ever-changing conditions. For this reason, bots are most effective when they are part of a well-thought-out strategy managed by a team of experts. This is where the combination of bots and copy trading becomes particularly powerful.

Indeed, when you copy a master trader using advanced automated trading bots, you are essentially gaining access to a powerful tool that may otherwise be out of reach. These bots are designed and continuously optimized by master traders, who dedicate substantial time and resources to ensure peak performance. Master traders, indeed, frequently update and fine-tune their bots to adapt to evolving market conditions. This allows you to leverage a cutting-edge trading system without bearing the high costs of development and maintenance. Instead, you simply share a portion of the profits—a worthwhile trade-off if the system delivers consistent returns. The beauty of copy trading in this scenario is that you get all the benefits of a sophisticated trading bot, but without the upfront costs, maintenance or technical know-how typically required.

Extra: Crypto Go Wealth Accelerator

After finishing this book, you might think:

"Alright, I get it. Now I know how to implement Value Investing, invest in ETFs, and use Day Trading to make money both in the long term and the short term... but it takes so much effort! Do I really need to spend that much time and energy?"

Unfortunately, the answer is yes. If you have a job or a business that demands most of your time, you may find it challenging to dedicate the necessary effort to long-term investing and short-term trading. Researching stocks or crypto assets, conducting analyses, and managing your portfolio require constant attention—not only to identify the best opportunities but also to know when to buy, when to sell, and how to rebalance your holdings effectively. **You can achieve meaningful results only by dedicating time every single day to monitoring markets, evaluating investment and trading opportunities, and refining your strategies.** This is the only way to maximize returns, minimize risks, and ensure you don't enter or exit at the wrong time.

But what if you don't have the time to do all of this every day? Are you wondering, *"Is there a faster and effortless way?"*

Our answer for you is Crypto Go Wealth Accelerator!

If you've made it this far, it's clear that you're looking for the most effective and effortless way to succeed in both short-term speculation and long-term investing. **Combining short-term trading profits with long-term investments is the ultimate strategy to accelerate your wealth.**

That's exactly what *Crypto Go Wealth Accelerator* **delivers—with minimum effort and maximum results!**

What Do We Offer?

By joining, you gain lifetime access to three powerful tools:

1. Smart Money Crypto Signals

Get lifetime access to 1 to 2 high-potential crypto signals per week, carefully selected based on Smart Money movements. No guess-work, no stress—just clear entry and exit points, making it easy to execute trades with confidence.

These signals are powered by both advanced on-chain analysis and deep fundamental research, ensuring you always stay ahead of the market. Our best-selling book, *"Cryptocurrency Investing"*, explains our methodology step by step. You can purchase it on Amazon to gain a deeper understanding. However, just like the techniques explained in this book, applying these strategies manually requires significant time and effort. With *Crypto Go Wealth Accelerator*, we take it a step further—removing all the complexity and effort for you. **We identify hidden crypto gems and provide precise entry and exit strategies—all you have to do is follow along.**

2. Crypto Short-Term Copy Trading with Bots

Let our proven strategies work for you—for life! Invest once, and our automated system will mirror every move we make. No experience needed—just set it up and watch your crypto grow with 24/7 trading bots that capitalize on market trends, even while you sleep. With automated crypto copy trading, your trades are executed automatically through a trusted broker, ensuring seamless execution without charts to analyze or stress to manage—just results. Our battle-tested strategies focus on highly capitalized assets like BTC and ETH, which are ideal for automated trading. This approach allows you to invest in BTC or ETH long-term while staying protected during bearish markets—ensuring you can make money even in downturns. **While our trading signals help you spot early-stage crypto gems, this strategy lets you profit from larger, more stable cryptocurrencies—effortlessly and automatically.**

3. ETF Long-Term Copy Investment

Get lifetime access to a diversified, expert-managed ETF portfolio designed for steady, sustainable growth. No effort required—just long-term wealth building made simple.

You can enjoy consistent annual returns without the volatility and stress of highly speculative markets. In this book, we've explained how you can invest long-term using both Value Investing and ETFs. However, if you're a lazy investor and want to completely outsource the creation, management, and rebalancing of your long-term portfolio, this service provides extraordinary value. **By leveraging this strategy, you eliminate the time and effort required to select the right assets, rebalance your portfolio, and apply all the principles we've discussed in this book—allowing you to grow your wealth effortlessly.**

Our Unbeatable Guarantee

We are so confident in our bestselling service, recognized worldwide by industry experts, that we offer an unbeatable guarantee:

If you don't receive at least one profitable signal (entry + exit) within the first 15 days of your purchase, you can request a FULL refund—no questions asked.

Learn More About Crypto Go Wealth Accelerator

Crypto Go Wealth Accelerator is available only a few times a year for new members. Discover all the details by scanning this QR code:

Conclusion

Dear reader, as we come to the end of this journey together, take a moment to reflect on how far you've come. You've equipped yourself with the tools, insights, and strategies to confidently step into the worlds of both long-term investing and short-term speculation. Let's take a quick look back at what you've learned:

- **The Barriers to Investing.** Why so many people never start investing (and are wrong not to) and how to overcome the fear of losing money.

- **The Financial Basics.** From understanding what investing truly means to distinguishing between speculation and long-term wealth creation. You've also learned about risk tolerance, building a cash emergency fund, and harnessing the power of compound interest.

- **The Investment Landscape.** Practical insights into stocks, ETFs, bonds, commodities, cryptocurrencies, and other key investment opportunities to consider for your portfolio.

- **Value Investing.** What value investing is, the key principles that drive it, essential metrics to identify undervalued stocks, and a step-by-step guide to applying DCF analysis to uncover stocks with great potential.

- **The Power of ETFs.** What ETFs are, their different types, unique benefits, and why they're an exceptional choice for a lazy investor's long-term portfolio.

- **Building and Managing a Balanced Portfolio.** Practical steps to create and maintain a well-diversified portfolio, including strategies like DCA, portfolio rebalancing, and tax-efficient techniques to maximize your returns.

- **Day Trading.** What day trading is, the best-suited assets, the basics of technical analysis, and popular strategies—along with an honest look at why day trading isn't the right choice for most people.

- **Alternatives to Day Trading.** Finally, we explored smarter options to day trading, including trading signals, copy trading, and trading bots.

I encourage you to revisit the chapters, reflect on the concepts, and put the strategies into action. Whether you're building a diversified portfolio or exploring short-term speculation, remember that patience and consistency will always be your greatest allies. In addition, keep in mind that the world of investing and trading is constantly evolving. Stay curious, stay informed, and never stop learning—these qualities will set you apart.

If you have any questions or doubts, don't hesitate to reach out to us at info@thecryptogo.com. Before we say goodbye, I'd like to ask a small favor. If you enjoyed this book, please leave us a review on Amazon by scanning the QR code below with your smartphone. Your support means the world to us!

I hope we'll have the opportunity to connect again in the future. In the meantime, I wish you all the best in achieving your investment and speculation goals.

Warm regards.

Bibliography

- **Bogle, J.C. (2017).** *The Little Book of Common Sense Investing: The Only Way to Guarantee Your Fair Share of Stock Market Returns.* Wiley.

- **Buffett, W. (2016).** *Berkshire Hathaway Annual Shareholder Letter.*

- **Buffett, W. (2019).** *The Essays of Warren Buffett: Lessons for Corporate America.* Edited by Lawrence A. Cunningham, 5th ed., Wiley, 2019.

- **Damodaran, A. (2012).** *Investment Valuation: Tools and Techniques for Determining the Value of Any Asset (3rd ed.).* Wiley.

- **Graham, B. (2006).** *The Intelligent Investor: The Definitive Book on Value Investing.* Revised Edition. Harper Business.

- **Kahneman, D. & Tversky, A. (1979).** *Prospect Theory: An Analysis of Decision under Risk.* Econometrica, 47(2), 263–291.

- **Malkiel, B. G. (2020).** *A Random Walk Down Wall Street: The Time-Tested Strategy for Successful Investing.* W.W. Norton & Company.

- **Mishkin, F. S. (2007).** *The Economics of Money, Banking, and Financial Markets.* Pearson Education.

- **S&P Dow Jones Indices (2021).** *SPIVA U.S.* Year-End 2021: Scorecard.

- **Vanguard Group. (2022).** *The Case for Index-Fund Investing.* Vanguard Research.

Made in the USA
Columbia, SC
22 April 2025